Mystery Shopping

2-Volume Set

(Includes the complete books of

The Perfect Work-At-Home Job: Mystery Shopping &

How-To Finally Make Money As A Mystery Shopper

By

Melanie R. Jordan

Mystery Shopping: 2-Volume Set
ISBN: 978-1-60145-396-9

Published By
SunLover Publishing

e-mail: Melanie@mysteryshoppercoach.com

Perfect Work-At-Home Job Update free monthly e-mail
subscription e-mail:
mscoach@aweber.com

Mystery Shopper Coach's Corner Web Site:
http://www.mysteryshoppercoach.com

SunLover Publishing publishes books on a number of "how-to"
topics that empower its readers related to work-at-home
lifestyles, infopreneuring, marketing and health and fitness.
Check out our web site at http://www.SunLoverPublishing.com
for other publications that you may enjoy.

Melanie R. Jordan may be contacted by e-mail using the
information provided above regarding this book (including
permission to reproduce selections). Your comments,
questions and suggestions are welcome.

Disclaimer

This book offers information on the subject matter indicated by the title. It is not intended to substitute for legal or other professional advice. Readers should consult with a professional whenever expert advice is needed. As laws and regulations may change from time to time, it is recommended that readers contact the appropriate authority to assure compliance with applicable statutes.

The author and publisher shall assume no responsibility or liability with respect to any loss or damage caused, or alleged to be caused, by the application of the information contained in this book.

If you feel a need to share this book, please do so with a reputable newsletter for review. Please don't copy it to give away. You're getting the benefit of my experience, which will give you a nice work-at-home income forever if you so desire, at a very reasonable price. Please allow me to earn a living so I can continue to create valuable books for you.

This book is dedicated to the world's best husband—my husband, Rich—for his complete support in my quest to become the writer I always knew I could be. As always, "thank you for loving me".

The Perfect Work-At Home Job: Mystery Shopping

By

Melanie R. Jordan

Fourth Edition 2007, Revised 11/07

Table of Contents

My Story

Ever do some surfing on the Internet and actually discover something worthwhile? That's how I first found out about Mystery Shopping, a.k.a. (also known as) Secret Shopping, a.k.a. Field Research, a.k.a Service Evaluation. I was a mystery shopper—first to supplement my income in sales which fluctuated wildly. One month I had money coming in, the next, someone changes their mind about a purchase and "poof"—no income! I was looking for a way to supplement what I was earning, while evening out the peaks and valleys, and stumbled upon what I then felt was "The Perfect Work-At-Home Job".

I am a former Vice President of Marketing for one of the country's top financial corporations who got caught up in a consolidating industry and a merger of giants. For all my hard work, I received the old "terminated due to merger", a.k.a. layoff, a.k.a. downsized, a.k.a. "thanks for your eight years of service and loyalty, don't let the door hit you in the butt on the way out".

Since then, while I did make additional attempts to stay in Corporate America, I found myself asking more and more frequently—"why"? Finally, I made up my mind to create a work life that allowed me to work out of a home-based office on my own schedule. <u>My work had to fit my life, not the other way around</u>.

So I became self-employed doing home-based financial services sales. For awhile it seemed like a good choice given my former corporate background except I discovered one thing—while I did well in sales, it just wasn't what I wanted to do solely in life. Well, at least I got the home-based part right, and ultimately it led to self-employed work as a marketing and infopreneur consultant —-much more in line with my love of helping others succeed. But it was at the time I did sales myself that I needed something else to do to bring in some "pocket money" to help me during the down times that are a given in the sales field for my bills and living expenses.

So as I said, one day, by surfing the internet, I stumbled upon the concept of Mystery Shopping from a link that led to another link, that led to another link (you know how that goes). Since then, I have found a way to regularly bring in some money without upfront investment whenever I need it, without going back to school and without people calling my former employers for references (not that I have bad ones, but it's nobody's business what I choose to do). I'd found my "Perfect Work-At-Home Job"!

How This Book Will Help You Become The Best Possible Mystery Shopper

Not to take away anything from other mystery shopping books that are out there (I believe you can learn something from everyone), but I found most of them had very little of the "in the trenches" insight that I am going to share with you. Most relied heavily on publishing lists of companies to contact. The players keep changing, and it's important to get the latest information which you can get for free very easily off the internet, and I will share with you how. Plus, applying to a couple of hundred companies is not, in my opinion, the best way to get mystery shopping work today.

Other books also focused on giving you forms for shops and long lists of what to look for on the shop which is really useless information. Every company—even for the same type of shop—will require you to fill out their own report forms and will have their own way to approach an assignment. There are some freebie tips posted here and there on the internet, but nothing that is this comprehensive that "tells it like it really is" and helps you become a professional mystery shopper who is in high demand getting the higher paying gigs, not just free hamburgers! Finally, the internet has changed this industry, and made becoming a mystery shopper easier than ever before. I'll take you by the hand and show you how the business works today online.

In this book, you'll learn:

- how to get your first jobs for real without spending

- your valuable time applying to hundreds of companies;

- how to go through the "middlemen" of the industry to have a better chance of getting assignments on a regular basis (and have them *coming to you*);

- how to stand out from the crowd and keep yourself in high demand;

- what type of assignments are worth your time, which are not (and if they are not, how to make them worthwhile)—includes the new trends in mystery shopping—digital, audio and video shops;

- strategies to get organized;

- how to complete your shops quickly so you can get in more shops and make more money while still "wowing" your clients;

- the 6 must-have pieces of e-mail correspondence you need to create to get jobs and make connections;

- 13 things you need to make it as a mystery shopper;

- 9 steps to performing mystery shops to make sure you do a great job, so you can get another job;

- 10 ways to maximize your mystery shopper income;

- *and so much more that it's time to stop listing everything and get you into the "meat" of this book.*

While I have geared this publication to the beginning mystery shopper, I also feel that shoppers with some experience who aren't making the money they feel they should can also benefit—especially those who do not have experience with complex service category assignments. I believe that one good idea that lands you an assignment, or results in a connection for work that you didn't have before, is always worthwhile. You'll probably earn back more than the cost of this book with your first assignment within days, or maybe even hours, of reading this book! From then on, you'll have "The Perfect Work-At-Home Job" and a way to earn money on your own schedule forever.

And if you haven't purchased this book as part of my *Mystery Shopping 2-Volume Set*, as an experienced shopper, you should definitely get my book written with you in mind called *How-To Finally Make Money As A Mystery Shopper*. It's available 24/7 at http://www.mysteryshoppercoach.com/books.html.

Mystery shopping companies generally don't offer true training to their shoppers, and if they do, it's usually specific to that company's needs, and they certainly don't teach you how to maximize your income as a mystery shopper (since you would need to work for many different companies). But I won't leave you hanging after you have finished this book.

You can also subscribe to my free e-zine *Perfect Work-At-Home Job Update* (former National Center For Professional Mystery Shoppers (NCPMS) Winner Best Newsletter) by sending an e-mail to me at mscoach@aweber.com. In my e-zine I answer select questions from my readers and share some of my latest tips and news from the trenches—*the inside scoop that you've been looking for, but no one tells you.* Also be sure to regularly check out my web site Mystery Shopper Coach's Corner at http://www.mysteryshoppercoach.com, for back issues of my e-zine, tips, resources, special offers and more!

Chapter One: So What Is Mystery Shopping Anyway?

It's not a secret that we live in a fiercely competitive business environment. Competing retailers open up the same type of store across the street from each other all the time. There are areas where there are four gas stations sitting on each of the four corners of a busy intersection. There are tons of places to get a hamburger. K-Mart®, Wal-Mart® and Target will all open within a few blocks of each other. If you are in a city or major suburb, there will be multiple apartment complexes competing for renters. Car dealers tend to all be on the same street. Several major hotels and motels cluster together for your vacation or business stay dollars. The list goes on and on.

What do all these businesses need to do to try and beat out the competition? Top quality companies who want to be around for many years to come do ongoing market research into their customers' experiences. They want to know if their employees are:

- treating customers well;

- doing their best to increase sales by suggesting additional items or services to purchase;

- following up on prospective customers to keep business going strong;

- keeping their stores or facilities well-maintained;

- looking well-groomed;

- presenting the company and its products or services in the best possible light;

- placing emphasis on the things that the company wants prospective customers to know;

- providing a positive experience that will keep customers coming back and encourage their referrals;

- sufficiently trained to do their jobs well;

- keeping them in compliance with any government regulations or local ordinances;

- maintaining proper business hours;

- answering the phone properly, pleasantly and promptly; and

- truly outstanding, or poor performers that should be replaced.

These are all pieces of information that are pure gold to any business that cares about its future and wants to do its best to stay ahead of the competition.

Now if the business owner or another employee tries to get the real story on what customers are experiencing on a regular basis at different times and on various days, it becomes difficult to do. If you know you are going to be monitored, you will of course be at your best that day (at least you would hope so). Plus, even if a company sent an employee who is not well known from another location, if that same person keeps stopping in, the employee will be tipped off. Another problem is that a company may not have enough employees who are "anonymous" to work with. Finally, an employee from the same company may be reluctant to rate a fellow employee poorly; may possibly rate a good employee poorly if he/she is having problems with that person; or even fail to tell the company something negative about its operations that may be difficult for "Corporate" to hear. Companies may succeed short-term with internal mystery shopping efforts, but long-term it's tough.

So how does a company get objective eyes and ears? They turn to specialized companies to handle the research—they may be market research companies who do all types of research studies including field or mystery shopping; private investigator or security firms; and, most frequently, companies dedicated to offering mystery shopping services to clients in need. For the same reason I mentioned above—different, objective people are constantly needed to pull off this research unknown to the employee—mystery shopping and other research companies need a steady stream of new faces and voices to conduct these assignments, jobs or "shops" as they are popularly called. That's where you and I come in. We are those faces and voices.

Chapter One: Notes/Questions

Chapter Two: What Does A Mystery Shopper Do?

Basically, depending upon the type of shop or research assignment, a mystery shopper, secret shopper, researcher, service evaluator, or most commonly referred to as simply "shopper" *will pretend in a believable fashion without giving away the fact they are a shopper, to be an actual customer or potential customer of a business.* In the process, the shopper will gather information and make observations that the client company wants to know about, and submit a report with their objective findings later on.

You may be asked to pretend you are looking for an apartment; interested in joining a gym; looking for cell phone service; or even considering buying a piano. Your job may be to rent a video; bring your car in for an oil change; have a meal; have a drink at a bar; go grocery shopping; etc. You could be asked to call a mail order house and evaluate its service, or even to check out a company's web site and see how easy you find it to use.

Almost any type of business—big or small, well-known chain or not—can use mystery shopping services. The types of shops you do can be as varied as you like, or you may decide to specialize only in certain kinds based upon your own personal preferences and the pay or work involved.

Chapter Two: Notes/Questions

Chapter Three: So Why Is Mystery Shopping The Perfect Work-At-Home Job?

There are many reasons why I feel this way—10 in fact:

1. You Can Work Out of a Home-based Office

Both you and the "middlemen" that are the key to getting many jobs will be working at home (when you are not out in the field doing an assignment of course). So there is no daily commute (reducing your stress level), and you gain time each day that you could use for better purposes like spending quality time with your spouse, significant other or kids. Plus, you can answer the phone in your pajamas if you like!

You also save on the expense of business attire—even if it's business casual, it's still expensive and not always very comfortable. I don't know about you, but I hate getting dressed up in business clothes. I was born and raised in New York City. As an adult trying to climb the corporate ladder, I had to get on the crowded subway in the middle of summer with the heat and humidity in a business suit and pantyhose. I feel awful just thinking about it! I am very fitness-oriented, so my main clothing designers are Reebok® and Everlast® and it suits me just fine (pun intended). The only time you may have to dress up a little is to look like a true customer for a dinner shop at an upscale restaurant or a business office space shop. Otherwise, casual—and not even business casual—is king!

2. You Can Work Your Own Schedule

If you want a three-day work week, it's yours! Prefer working only a couple of hours a day—go ahead! Need to take care of the kids? No problem! Want weekends off? You got it! Want to go to the gym in the middle of the day? Do it! Want a two-hour lunch? Why not? Want to take a week off to travel? There's no one to ask for time off but yourself!

3. You Are Your Own Boss

With the exception of a handful of companies I have come across, all mystery shopping companies that you will work with do so on an independent contractor basis. This means that you are not an employee of their company. In fact, they will usually have you sign a form or click an "I agree" statement on their web sites to be sure you understand this so you don't come to them looking for benefits. It also means that you are free to work for as many different companies as you please (as long as you keep your work for each client separate and confidential), and can accept or decline an assignment offered to you as you wish.

Just be sure that any independent contractor agreement that you sign for a company does not require that you work with them on an exclusive basis. Read the fine print. I personally have never seen this come up, because having an exclusivity requirement would likely go against the IRS definition of an independent contractor, but I have heard that it is something to look out for.

You don't want to do anything that limits your ability to do as many shops, for as many different companies as possible.

4. There is No Upfront Investment Required

This is not a business opportunity and you really don't need to pay anyone just to get an assignment or to join their company's database of shoppers. I have seen several directories that list available shoppers in which you pay to be included. And as mystery shopping companies try to fund their internet operations, many who were free are now charging shoppers to register on their site or give preferential status to those who do pay. While many such services are legitimate, I have not found it necessary.

Also, while we're on the subject, beware of scams. Some less than scrupulous individuals or companies take out ads in the jobs or business opportunities sections of local newspapers claiming they have a job for you as a mystery shopper. Call them, and it often turns out to be a recording where they just want to sell you a list of companies for a hefty amount. Or worse yet, it could lead you to accidentally become a victim to a long-distance phone scam where you press a number on your phone and the next thing you know, a bunch of calls to Guatemala and Columbia are billed to you. If you ever answer an ad, see if there is an option to respond by e-mail—it's the safest way to see if an ad is a legitimate opportunity.

This is now primarily an on-line business, and to the best of my knowledge, the best companies and middlemen rarely, if ever, use classified ads to recruit shoppers. I myself have only come across one classified newspaper ad that was legitimate. Almost every mystery shopping company has a web site, there are reliable lead boards where the "middlemen" post available assignments for the client companies they work with and you will most likely be contacted by e-mail. This is how it's done today.

5. It Does Not Take Much to Get Started

You ideally should have high-speed internet access, but you can get by with dial-up if need be. Whoever you currently use to access the internet, if they are reliable, that's fine. Of course, keep in mind that if you use a freebie service and you have trouble getting on-line to either find out about assignments, or to submit your completed reports, you could be missing out on potential income.

You will need an e-mail account. I suggest if you can, having a separate e-mail address or screen name (if on AOL) just for your mystery shopping work that is directed to you personally. You will eventually get a lot of e-mails representing an opportunity to earn money and you don't want them buried in with junk messages about "how to lose 20 pounds by tomorrow", an offer for a free psychic reading and the latest joke your best friend sent you. You also don't want a dual name or family name e-mail address (i.e. jackanddiane@xyz.com or smithfamily@xyz.com so you can be taken seriously. Also avoid inappropriate names like loverboy@xyz.com.

Act like a professional. You'll then be treated like one and get more assignments offered to you than you can handle!

Most households have their own computer which certainly is helpful. Plus using it to create income may make part of the computer's cost a tax deduction for you—ask your tax advisor. Any way you have to easily and regularly get computer access will work. You don't need fancy software, *but you should have some form of word processing software (yes Microsoft® Word is the typical standard), and ideally Microsoft® Excel spreadsheet software* (many forms used for shops are pre-formatted in this popular software format by the mystery shopping companies and their clients).

If you don't have Excel, some companies will fax you forms and still give you the assignment. But if you fax in reports, you will often be paid less for the assignment because the company will have to re-type your report to edit and compile it for their clients. You also might not get an assignment if you don't have the ability to work with Excel documents, so try not to give yourself a disadvantage if you can help it. By the way, you do not have to be a computer whiz or know how to make a spreadsheet, you simply need to know how to enter data and save it—the mystery shopping company or middleman will send you the formatted document.

There are only two other software programs you need to know about:

- WinZip®
  It is used to open zip files (what else) for PC users. WinZip may be needed to open up larger or multiple documents that have been compressed for e-mailing to speed up the amount of time they take to download. It is a freebie that you can download from www.winzip.com (click on the latest demo version).

- Adobe Acrobat® Reader

  If you didn't buy this book as a pdf file, then you need to know about this software. Some forms or documents to be read like company-specific training materials, or guidelines for the particular shop, may be in a format that is made with Adobe software that creates what is known as a "pdf" file. You need to be able to access such files that are sent to you or that you are asked to view on a company's web site. This is another freebie available at www.adobe.com. If you try to open a document that is in pdf format, the software senses this and automatically opens it for you—it's as simple as that.

You should also have printer access to print out your reports for your records, and copies of forms that are e-mailed to you to be used for your shops (if you can handle Excel forms).

You do not absolutely have to have your own fax, as long as you have fax access somehow through a local UPS® Store or other source, a fax program in your computer or one of the fax services on the internet like Efax®. Even if you e-mail all your reports, unless you have a scanner (you don't need one), when you must send in receipts from a shop or a business card as proof of going to the assignment site, you have to copy and fax them in. Also, there are still some companies who work with faxed reports. They will fax the assignment to you and you will fax it back (no penalty in the amount you are paid), so fax access is needed.

You don't need a separate phone line, although I have VoIP service (uses cable or DSL line access for phone calls vs. a wired traditional phone line) through a top supplier. *You should have voicemail.* I find that every company is different in how they work with you—some will use e-mail; many use the phone and mail. You will want to be able to get their messages in a reliable way—not missing the call or having to count on anyone else in your household to take down the right message. Voicemail sounds professional and it's usually very cheap (or like in the case of my VoIP service, it's free with the service). Make sure that any voicemail service you use allows you to have a separate mailbox just for your calls so they are not buried in with your teenager's. Also, your line will never be busy so that a caller with a potential job for you cannot get through.

Whatever method you use, make a professional recording like *"you've reached the office of _____. Please leave a message with the best time to return your call and*

I'll get back to you as soon as possible. Thank you for calling." No background music; no babies wailing; no joint recordings with your kid, boyfriend, girlfriend or spouse; and no cutesy jokes or other voices. Again, be a professional, even if you are working at home. In fact, go overboard to act professional, as home-based workers often are not taken seriously (jealousy from those who trudge into an office I suppose). You do not want to give anyone a reason to have this perception.

If you have a cell phone (and these days who doesn't), that is very helpful as you can get calls for another assignment (handled tactfully of course), while you are working a job! Again, keep it professional—don't have one of those songs that answer the phone first delaying access to you from someone who is thinking of offering you an assignment!

Finally, *you need access to a reliable, insured car, or if you live in a major city like New York, access to easy mass transit* (in a city, a car may not be necessary and it actually can become a hindrance). Most shops will not be within walking distance, so you'll need to drive to them. How many miles you are willing to drive is up to you. Keep in mind that most shops will not include reimbursement for your mileage (but mileage may be tax deductible to you—check with your tax advisor).

When accepting assignments you need to keep in mind your gas mileage and how much it costs you to travel a certain distance. If necessary, drop some areas you will shop, or require multiple assignments in the same area to make it worth the gas.

Your time is a factor as well. When I was living in Southern California doing mystery shopping, you had to drive just about everywhere. Because of traffic and the sheer volume of cars on the road, it could take you quite awhile to get where you're going. You have to decide how much drive time that you could be using for other assignments, other work you do, or for living your life, you are willing to give up for each assignment.

6. You Can Live Just About Anywhere

You don't have to live in a major area or in a particular state to do mystery shopping work. In fact, you will likely get your assignments from middlemen and mystery shopping companies that are not even located in your state! I see assignment postings for every state in the United States and other countries. There are requests for suburban areas, small towns, and resort areas. I love it when I see a listing for Hawaii—I think to myself, how lucky are they? I also have seen companies that do shops in Canada. A posting even came up through one of my regular job lead sources for an assignment in London (no travel reimbursement of course). Please note that I am writing this book based on my knowledge of mystery shopping in the United States, but I'll have some tips later that are geared towards those of you who live in Canada and other foreign countries.

So if you move, or perhaps are retired and spend part of the year in another part of the country, no problem. You just update your profiles with companies and middlemen and start doing shops where you are.

7. <u>You Can Use it As a Means to An End</u>

Perhaps you're like me and are aspiring to do something new with your life. For me, it is writing and personal coaching on topics I have knowledge of, experience in, and am passionate about. I am working towards making a very sizable living in these two endeavors, and I want to make sure I have the time to really become successful. Mystery shopping is the most flexible and non-interfering work I know of. So by doing mystery shopping, you have the chance to make money as you need it without having to get a job with a set schedule; fixed hours; workdays that may not fit in with your schedule; a fixed amount you can earn; trouble getting time off; having a boss; commuting; getting dressed up; etc.

As a reader of this book, maybe you're an aspiring actor, you're in school or want to go back to school, you're starting or have started a new business that isn't quite bringing in what you want it to yet, you want to stay at home with your kids, or you're retired and looking for a few bucks plus a way to stay busy. Perhaps you need a second job, you're saving for something special like a dream vacation, you're paying off some debts, or you want to free up time to do volunteer work.

Maybe you just got laid-off from work with a limited severance package, or no severance package, and need some money coming in while you look for another job. Whatever your reasons, mystery shopping can play a role in supplementing your income (or lack of) while you work on getting where you really want to be. Or it can simply be good steady money that fits in with the life you lead.

8. It's Interesting Work That is Always Different

Do you get bored easily? I do. When I look back at the shops I have done, I am truly amazed at how many different industries and companies I have done assignments for. One day I test-drove a sports car. The next, I shopped for an apartment in a place I could not possibly otherwise afford. And on the next, I got to eat at my favorite restaurant for free!

When I was in Corporate America, companies always wanted to pigeonhole you into working in an industry in which you already had experience and didn't want to let you market software if you came from banking (I did actually eventually get to make that crossover during my career, but it was tough). There is no such stigma here. You can immediately obtain work in any industry and for all different companies—plus, you are not penalized for "job-hopping"! In fact, that's the way things are.

As a side benefit, for a creative person like me, it is good for the imagination to do so much role playing. It's also great for your conversational and people skills.

9. Your Opinion Counts and You Get Paid For It

I can't stand poor customer service. It drives me up the wall. I am one of those people who will bother to write or e-mail a company's CEO, or the manager of a store or hotel if I have a legitimate complaint. In fairness, I am also the same person who will let a company know if an employee provides great service, or goes above and beyond the call of duty for me. Plus, I also like to make suggestions. Guess what? All of these are things you can get paid for as a mystery shopper.

Generally, you will be asked in the report you make to just state the facts of what you observed and noticed during the assignment. However, there is always a section at the end where you are asked for your opinion. Companies want to know about how their place of business was maintained and if any employees were either exemplary, rude or poorly groomed. I always root for employees to do a good job so they will hopefully get rewarded when my report is filed. Yet when an employee really does a poor job, I can't help but think "you picked the wrong person to do that to today"!

10. It Can Help Stretch Your Budget

While you can accumulate some nice money from the fees paid to you for doing mystery shopping on a regular basis (more on this later), you also have to take into consideration that you get a lot of things for free that you might otherwise have to pay for out of your own pocket. By doing mystery shopping, you can actually make your household budget go further, and possibly even get to do things you would not otherwise get to do as often, if at all.

For example, an assignment is available for a dinner shop at a nice restaurant in your area. Usually the reimbursement for this would cover dinner for two (not many people dine alone so it looks better to have two people dining together). In fact, you may be told specifically that at least one of you must order a drink, have an appetizer, an entrée and dessert—all amounts

covered by the shop reimbursement. So you got a free dinner in exchange for a report—maybe even one in a place that you couldn't normally afford!
Or a little less exotic, but no less helpful in stretching your budget, is an oil change assignment. I love this because the company I work with regularly on this assignment pays for the oil change *plus* they pay you a shop fee for doing the shop and simple report.

It's easy to see how you could actually increase your standard of living by doing mystery shopping both from the money you make and the freebies you get. You were going to get your oil changed at some point anyway, right (I hope)? So now you got it paid for *and someone paid you to do a task you would have done as part of your normal life.* Get the idea? Not bad! Try to choose assignments that would pay for items or services you would have bought anyway and/or pay you to do so.

Chapter Three: Notes/Questions

Chapter Four: What Does It Take To Make It As A Mystery Shopper?

First of all anyone can be a mystery shopper—male or female, young or old, fat or skinny, tall or short, any race or religion. Most assignments are open to anyone that is believable as a potential customer. You can be 18 and shop a fast food place, but you would not be believable as a retirement community shopper. Or if you wear a size 10 and are asked to shop in a Plus size store, it wouldn't work at all.

I have seen bank shops that required you to be within a certain age range to match the profile of an investment account customer. Sometimes you need to have a child or access to one to be believable for a shop like a day care center. Some assignments for eating establishments or banks will request a certain ethnic background or the ability of the shopper to speak another language to make sure a company's employees do not discriminate. You can help bring about social change! See how important you are?

Here is a list of 13 qualities (such a lucky number, I know) that I feel you need to make it as a shopper. If you need to work on some of them, keep at it and you'll get better in time.

1. Maintains Anonymity

This does not mean that you do not give your name (although it will sometimes be a made-up name) when you do a shop. *It means that you never, ever reveal that you are a shopper either by your actions in completing the assignment or by confirming it if asked.* That's why it is usually referred to as mystery or secret shopping—no one can know that you are not a real customer!

2. Follows Instructions

There is a reason why the guidelines for an assignment will be written a certain way, or why a client asks a particular question indicating they want you to be on the lookout for that piece of information. They are paying for the research and the mystery shopping company is paying you to do what their clients want. If you don't do what is asked, you are ruining the research, you won't get paid and you won't get an assignment again from that company.

3. Is Observant

You are being paid to notice what is going on and your interaction with one or more employees. You must be able to look for whatever details the assignment requires. Many assignments require being able to make observations about things you would not normally bother to remember. Was the employee wearing a nametag? Exactly how long did it take to get my food? How much are they charging for the Super Texter model cell phone? When you're getting paid to be aware of these small points though, you will be!

4. Good Memory

Since you are pretending to be a customer or prospective customer, it would be a dead giveaway if you took notes while doing your assignment unless it can be done very discreetly. Even then you may be taking a chance on getting spotted as a shopper. You need to get good at remembering what happened; in what order; major characteristics of people you interact with (i.e. ethnic background, hair color, glasses or no, approximate height, what they were wearing); and if the things the company asked you to observe were in place (like a promotional display).

5. Is Reliable

When you take on an assignment, the company or middlemen are counting on you to do it correctly and to meet the deadline they have established. If you get a reputation for not delivering, doing sloppy assignments, or getting pegged as a shopper, you won't get any more work from that company. I am amazed at the number of cancellations and failures to do shops that you see from the frantic e-mails and postings of middlemen on a regular basis. (Note—you can use this to your advantage as I'll explain later).

6. Is Honest

You are not creating a fictional story when you report on a shop. You need to state the facts of what happened. You can't withhold something that occurred because you feel sorry for the employee and you know that word will get back to the company. You can't skip going to the shop location, try to say you went and make up a report. Not only will this be obvious from your lack of detail, but the companies have ways to monitor whether you actually did the shop or not. They can check guest cards at a gym, require a business card or ask for the floor plan of an apartment. I have even heard of some video surveillance tapes for the business establishment that were in operation anyway used to verify shopper activity when this question arose. If you don't provide an accurate report, you won't get paid. You could be asked to do the shop over (if possible) for free, and you will jeopardize your chances of getting future assignments.

7. <u>Has Good Communication Skills</u>

You don't have to be a great conversationalist, but you do need the basics. You must be able to carry on a conversation and ask questions that would make sense if you really were a customer or prospect of the business. You have to be able to write well enough to complete a report, but you don't have to have perfect grammar, be a spelling champion (that's what word processing spell check is for) or be a screenwriter.

8. <u>A Good Imagination</u>

You don't have to go for an Oscar® caliber performance in doing your shops, but you need to think ahead before you go out to do the assignment so you are believable and your "story" comes out naturally. Imagine yourself as a real customer or prospect for this particular company and act appropriately. For example, if you really were buying a piano, what would you want to know? If you were going to join a gym, what do you think they might ask so you could prepare your answers in advance?

9. <u>Acts professionally</u>

As you probably noticed already, I have asked you to be a professional so you get treated as one. It makes a difference, and helps you stand out from the crowd so you get contacted first for an assignment. I'll give many more tips on how to accomplish this, so keep reading.

10. <u>Is Well-Organized</u>

My husband would laugh really hard at this. All things being equal, I will never be organized when clutter will do. But when there is money at stake, I can be the most organized person around!

For documentation purposes, until you get paid, you need to keep copies of your reports, receipts, materials given to you during the shop, business cards, etc. in case your report or a receipt gets misplaced and you need to re-submit it. It is also helpful to have examples of past reports to help refresh your memory the next time you do an assignment for that company or type of business.

You need to keep track of each assignment's due dates and any notes about what days or hours to do the shop. Most importantly, since you will likely be working with several companies and doing many shops each month, you need to keep track of your report submissions, when payment is due and if you received payment.

I have been fortunate in that so far no one has ever failed to pay me what I was due for an assignment (although I have heard that while it is rare, it has happened). I did discover twice through my record keeping when I had a payment that was quite overdue. I contacted the companies and they apologized and sent immediate payment. But had I not kept track, I could have missed out on receiving the money I had earned. I have a handy Excel spreadsheet that I use to track my payments that I would be happy to send you for free if you e-mail me at Melanie@mysteryshoppercoach.com.

11. Thinks on Their Feet

Since you are involved in a real transaction or situation with one or more employees, things don't always go the way you planned. You have to expect the unexpected and quickly change gears if your scenario isn't working, or you aren't getting the information you are being paid to gather.

For example, I had a gym shop where I said I wanted to join that particular location because I just got offered a job at company ABC a couple of blocks away. I thought this was a good scenario to explain why I was interested in joining a gym that was about 20 miles away from where I lived. To my surprise, the employee I was shopping then said that I should wait because company ABC would have a corporate rate and he couldn't help me. I would have to sign up through them.

I was in danger of losing the opportunity to get the shop in. I stalled for a second and said "well, I believe I am going to go work for them, but I also have another offer from a smaller company in the area and haven't decided which I am going with. I may very well just join by myself, so could you please tell me more about your memberships?" See what I mean about being quick on your feet? The employee went into his pitch, showed me the club, and I got my assignment done properly.

12. Maintains Objectivity

You must set aside your personal opinions when you do a shop. For example, you may personally hate pushy salespeople (I never was one), but it may be exactly what the client wants their salespeople to do. You may go to a fast food place and not like the food you ordered, but the item was required for the shop. You shouldn't let that influence your answers on whether or not the food was warm; the lettuce was wilted; or if the employee gave you the correct change.

13. Has Basic Internet/Computer Knowledge

As I mentioned earlier, you don't need to be a computer geek, but when it comes to the internet, you should know how to send and receive e-mail; how to work with attachments; and how to access web sites. Basic computer skills should include word processing, the ability to fill in data on forms created with Microsoft Excel and knowing how to create and save documents. That's it!

Chapter Four: Notes/Questions

Chapter Five: How Much Money Can I Make? Can I Quit My Day Job?

First, I will not mislead you and say you can make $50,000 a year doing mystery shopping—at least not unless you own a mystery shopping company. How much you make will depend on how many shops you do each week or each month and the kinds of shops they are. For example, a fast food shop may only get you a free lunch. Or that same assignment might offer a reimbursement of $10 with a requirement to order a certain item, and you get to keep what's left so you net only $5 to $7 (not including the free food). That's not going to pay many bills.

Fortunately, many shops pay reasonably well and the key to your income is quantity, being smart about the jobs you accept and being organized (more on this later). The better paying jobs tend to be service-related and are more complex, or involve the use of some technology like audio/video taping or digital cameras. As you become more experienced, you'll do them quicker so you can make more money. You can expect most service-related shops to pay between $20 and $50 apiece; shops that use audio taping can go as high as $50 each, and video mystery shopping assignments have been known to offer up to $100 (this usually involves the use of your equipment when you hit the higher end of the range). Sometimes there are bonuses offered for beating deadlines or a rush job, and actual pay for shops in your area may vary.

Very simple shops may pay in the $5-10 range, but often these are retail shops where you are also making a purchase of a small item for which you are reimbursed. So you end up with a freebie that you were saved from paying for out of your own pocket. For example, I did a shop for a major book chain that paid $8, but I also had to buy a paperback book which I was reimbursed for up to $8. So I really got paid $16 for my work.

Simple shops may also be done in combination where you can make a nice overall amount. I did one at my local airport on a day when I had to drop my husband off for a business trip anyway. I got paid $15 to stop at the airport bar (before the gates) plus reimbursement for a free drink, and to visit the snack bar where I would have also gotten free food but it was closed when it was supposed to be open, so I got paid for the shop anyway. I was also reimbursed for tolls and parking. So for taking my husband to the airport which I had to do anyway, I made $22.50 in cash and merchandise (as they say on the game shows), for about 40 minutes work. It would have required even less of my time if I didn't have to wait for the official snack bar opening that never occurred anyway. Intermediate-level shops—where you go to a retail store, make many observations, try something on (if applicable) and interact with employees usually pay in the $12-$25 range.

So what's a complex shop? It is one that requires multiple actions like a retail store where you purchase an item, make some observations, leave and then come back an hour or two later to return the merchandise to test how well they handle returns. It can also be a service shop (like for an apartment shop) with multiple steps like a phone call and an on-site visit, or one that requires what is known as a narrative. This is when you must do more than fill in a simple yes or no answer to a question on a form. A couple of sentences explaining a "no" or "yes" answer will be required. Maybe a paragraph on each phase of your on-site visit is needed for a service shop. Or sometimes a full page must be written detailing everything about your experience, which is common for an apartment shop or a car dealer shop. Please see the Resource Section at the end of the book for an example of a detailed narrative.

Before you accept an assignment, you need to know how much of it is narrative versus "yes or no" or very simple, one sentence answers being required. This way, you will know if the pay is worth the effort that is expected. Also know that not all companies will pay the same for the same type of shop or level of effort. I have seen apartment shops, which are probably about the most complex type of shop, that paid as little as $15, while others paid $20, $25, $30 or even up to $50. They all required the same amount of effort, which is why you have to learn what is reasonable so you don't get taken advantage of.

Personally, now that I am experienced, I won't do a shop that pays under $20 unless:

- It is right in my immediate neighborhood, or another one that I visit regularly anyway, and is a quick "yes or no" check-off form without a narrative.

- It is an opportunity to get experience with a new type of shop.

- It is an opportunity to get "in" with a new company with whom I want to work.

- There is also a reimbursed freebie as part of the deal that makes the overall value $20 or more (and it is something I want or would actually use).

- It is an easy, no-narrative, regularly-occurring shop in my immediate neighborhood, or another one I visit regularly, so my monthly income from the job is worthwhile. Plus once you repeat a shop, you'll likely start doing it faster.

- I can combine one or more easy jobs in the same stop, so my overall stop is worth $20 or more. The time you would normally spend in travel time is eliminated, making a multi-shop stop, even if each shop is lower-paying, more worthwhile.

If there is a pretty good demand for shoppers in your area, it is entirely possible to make up to $1,000 in a month's time in actual cash and freebies depending upon the types of shops you do with a "full-time" effort. You also may be able to even double that figure to as much as $2,000 in a month's time in major markets, or reach it more regularly, by taking on video and audio mystery shopping work.

Other income boosters focus on complementary assignments such as report editing and scheduling work available to you as a more established shopper—a very experienced independent scheduler can make as much as $2,500 a month (see *Chapter Fourteen: How To Maximize Your Income As A Mystery Shopper By Standing Out From The Crowd—For Anyone New Or Experienced*). The more types of work you get involved with, the higher your income will be.

Of course, if you are in a rural area, don't count on reaching such an income level on shops alone because the number of possible businesses in your area available to be shopped is much smaller. On the other hand, your cost of living is likely a lot lower too. Then again, I have seen a lot of desperate requests for shoppers in more remote areas of Northern California that almost made me want to drive a few hundred miles because the pay was so good (well, maybe if they also paid for mileage). If you live in or on the outskirts of a major city, you should do well with the right amount of effort.

Despite what you may have heard, overall demand for mystery shoppers is great as companies realize the importance of staying competitive and providing a positive customer experience. You can work almost every day if you want to—if you get the word out about yourself properly; get a reputation for being reliable; are able to jump in at the last minute; and do solid, professional work.

If you figure an average of $25 earned per shop in cash and/or freebies, this would mean if you just do strictly mystery shopping, you need to do 40 shops per month to earn $1,000. For example, this could break down to an average of one a day for 30 days/two a day for 10 days, or two a day for 20 days. For the "one a day" schedule, figure that in the 10 cases where you need to do a second shop per day to hit your 40 shops per month goal, those could be restaurant shops. You wouldn't mind eating out in restaurants 10 times during the month would you? If you also did higher-paying audio and video shops, assuming an average of $50 for those, you could do just 25 shops and earn the same $1,000 (15 audio/video shops and 10 regular shops).

Generally, to keep the quality of your shops high, I do not recommend doing more than two or three complex shops in a day (although I have done four or five in a day on an emergency basis for high pay).

And when I say "full-time", I mean you are willing to do a shop or more a day, but a shop could take a half hour, a detailed, narrative report an hour, plus your travel time. This means you might have to work two hours a day, or maybe up to four hours a day to do two shops (timing varies by the shop type and your level of experience). I like that definition of full-time versus the standard eight hours or more most people think of! This gives full-time a whole new meaning!

Or if you just want to earn some extra money, you can easily make $400 to $500 per month in actual cash and freebies without working weekends or even every day! Again, figure at an average of $25 per traditional mystery shopping job, you need 16 jobs to make $400 cash (or just 8 shops if they were audio/video at $50 apiece).

Suppose you wanted to make $250 extra a month. Using a $25 average, that's just 10 traditional shops or 5 audio/video shops!

There also tends to be more work in the first few days of the month when new job orders come in to the middlemen, and at the end of the month when unfilled jobs run up against deadlines and shopper cancellations. Again, your actual earnings can be more or less depending upon the time you put in; where you live; and the type of shops you do. When you need more money, you can put in more time or change the types of shops you are willing to do.

If you have enough money to meet your needs in a particular month, you can kick back, go on vacation or work on whatever it is you are truly trying to do. I once took three weeks off while my Dad underwent surgery and I went to visit and help out in Florida. It was nice to have that freedom to drop everything and be where I was needed the most without having to beg anyone for time off.

When I came back, I wanted to get back into the swing of things and earn some money, so I took on nine jobs and earned $239.50 (all but $5 was cash) in eight days for an average of $29.94 per shop. If I kept that pace up for the month, I could have earned about $900. But I wanted to get back to my writing and coaching, and as one of my favorite live musical performers Eddie Money says in the song "It's Another Nice Day in L.A., *"I could get to the top but I don't want to work that hard"*. Besides I was about to go away for a long weekend with my husband and then back to Florida to visit my Dad again. But that's the beauty of it. <u>Make money when you want to on your terms, and don't when you have other things to do.</u>

So as you can see, there is money to be made, and free items and services that can be paid for that will certainly stretch your budget. You can get paid for doing things you would do anyway, and/or have items paid for that you would have bought anyway. But if you have a "real" day job, I wouldn't quit. Consider this your "Perfect Work-At-Home Second Job"—a way to supplement your primary job and stretch your budget.

For others, like someone who has been laid-off and needs cash while looking for another job; someone with savings trying to launch a business; creative-types like myself with an understanding husband who works; students; retired people; stay at-home Moms or Dads; or those who are just looking to earn extra money for their special vacation, this is your "Perfect Work-At-Home Job".

Chapter Five: Notes/Questions

Chapter Six: A Word About Getting Paid

When you are first starting out, it is important to note that as an independent contractor, you are not on a regular pay schedule. It's not as though you can count on receiving your "paycheck" every other Friday from your employer. If you do a shop on Wednesday, it does not mean you will get paid on Thursday or even next Thursday. Every single mystery shopping company has their own payment schedule. Most will pay either within 30 days of the shop or 15-30 days from the end of the month from which your shop was completed.

In the first case, if you do a shop on May 30th, it means your check will go out by June 30th. In the second case, it means that if you do a job on May 30th, your check could go out on June 15th or June 30th. This "lag time" in payment is due to the mystery shopping company having to compile and possibly edit down all the reports from their shoppers; present the final reports to their client; and address any questions or disputes regarding the information. Then they need to get their payment, so they can, in turn, pay you. Always know the company's policy on the timing of payments so you can plan your own budget accordingly.

Once you get up and running, and work fairly regularly as a shopper, these lags will take care of themselves as you will have built up a steady stream of checks (or credits to your PayPal™ account) coming your way. But know that when you first begin, you may not see the first money you earned for anywhere from 30-60 days. Be sure you have some funds in reserve or are still doing other work until the first checks come in.

Please also realize that your actual earnings will likely vary from month-to-month based on your effort; demand for shoppers in your area; and the number of higher-paying shops or shops with bonuses attached. Plus, you may hit into a waiting period to be eligible to do some shops again as required by the client. For example, it is common to have to wait six months before shopping the same apartment location again.

Chapter Six: Notes/Questions

Chapter Seven: A Word About Taxes

Let me start this section off with the disclaimer that I am not a tax professional, and that you should verify the following information with your own tax advisor as regulations are constantly changing, and everyone's tax situation is unique. Now that I have gotten that out of the way, here is a basic idea of what it means to be an independent contractor from a tax point-of-view.

First, you are considered self-employed, which means that you will receive a form 1099 at year-end to let the IRS know what you have earned rather than a W-2. Please note that the 1099 amount is reported to the IRS, but this does not necessarily mean, for example, that you have $1,000 worth of income when it says $1,000 on your 1099. This is because you may be entitled to deductions that reduce your amount of taxable income. By law, you are only required to receive a 1099 from those mystery shopping companies that have paid you $600 or more during the year. However, even if you don't receive a 1099, the income is still reportable. Schedule C is used to report self-employed income to the IRS when you do your taxes.

A bit of good news is that you do not have taxes withheld from each payment you receive for doing your shops. So if you earn $40 for a shop, you don't receive a check for $25 after withholding of taxes. The bad news is that you are responsible for paying all of your own social security taxes at year-end, if you show a profit, which are normally split between you and your employer. Also, you may need to pay quarterly estimated income taxes (your tax advisor can figure this out for you). But these are not additional taxes, they are the taxes you would have paid over the course of the year anyway.

Even better news is that as someone who is self-employed, there are many deductions available to you, that are not possible for someone who is employed. For example, when someone burns through their gas each day commuting to work, it is money they generally do not get to deduct—you probably can.

Here is a list of some of the possible deductions to which you may be entitled:

- mileage (if not reimbursed), or a percentage of your car's use for your mystery shopping work (this can include your car payment, repairs, maintenance)

- parking and tolls (if not reimbursed)

- business use of your home (a percentage of your rent or mortgage payment plus all utilities and insurance)

- telephone—cost of a second line, voicemail, phone calls (local and long distance related to your work)

- internet access—part or all of your dialup ISP, DSL or cable modem monthly service charge

- postage (if not reimbursed)

- office equipment and supplies—this can include a percentage of the cost of the item for the amount that you use it in your mystery shopping work.

- Items such as a computer, fax, scanner, printer, digital camera, calculator, answering machine, file cabinet, a desk and chair, those expensive laser and fax toner cartridges, paper, paper clips, etc. all could be at least partially tax deductible to you.

You and your tax advisor can likely think of other deductions to which you would be entitled, but I just wanted to give you a good idea of what was possible. Notice how this is another way that you enhance your standard of living because the government, through tax deductions, helps subsidize your housing cost, equipment, car costs, and more. That digital camera you wanted to buy to take pictures of the kids, or to use on your next vacation, is now likely to be partly deductible for the amount you use it in your mystery shopping work.

What happens is that by allowing these deductions, you can substantially reduce the amount of profit you have as a mystery shopper for tax purposes. You may even proportionally pay a lot less income tax than if you were a W-2 employee because some of your costs that are tax-deductible are subsidized by the government. You may also be able to set up a special type of retirement account for yourself (such as a SEP-IRA). Such accounts are designed for self-employed people to allow you to put away a greater proportion of income for retirement based on how much profit you have from being self-employed.

These accounts are also not available to W-2 employees and they can even further reduce your taxable income.

The end result is that each dollar you earn being self-employed could be worth a lot more to you than you think. Get yourself a good tax advisor if you don't have one already, or if you are a do-it-yourself type, get your hands on everything you can regarding self-employment and taxes.

Chapter Seven: Notes/Questions

Chapter Eight: A Word About Local Regulations

Whenever you start working as a self-employed person, it's always a good idea to check with your local authorities to make sure you are not violating any regulations. Since you are working out of your home, you want to make sure that there is no issue with zoning laws or even with your home owner's association (if you have one) regarding this use of your home.

In Southern California, it's a given that lots of people have home-based businesses or telecommute and work out of their home. It's actually encouraged—one less commuter on the crowded freeways. You can't look at a home or apartment over one bedroom and not have the agent tell you how a particular room will "make a wonderful home office". In other parts of the country, there may be some 100-year old zoning law on the books that you need to be aware of. Since you are not operating a business with employees that is in any way visible to your neighbors, or could possibly interfere with their daily living, it's likely not an issue. Still, it never hurts to be sure.

Also be certain that you do not need any kind of business permit or occupational license such as a private investigator license to do mystery shopping work. In California, the Business and Professions code, section 7522, specifically lists someone who does mystery shopping work as exempt from private investigator laws. It excludes:

> "A person or business engaged in conducting objective observations of consumer purchases of

products or services in the public environments of a business establishment by the use of a pre-established questionnaire, provided that person or business entity does not engage in any other activity that requires licensure pursuant to this chapter. The questionnaire may include objective comments."

I have heard however, that it is possible a state may require a private investigator license for mystery shopping work. Nevada does. So check on the rules in your state to know the facts and what would be required if you do need one. Do not rely on a mystery shopping company or scheduler to know this information. As an independent contractor, it's your responsibility to know the applicable laws. Plus, the addition of audio and video mystery shops to the assignment types now being done by mystery shoppers, may be considered to be beyond the scope of traditional work in that field by some jurisdictions.

A helpful web site I found with links regarding the private investigator laws in each state is www.crimetime.com/licensing.htm.

And if you do find that you need a license, you shouldn't let this stop you from doing mystery shopping. Many businesses and professions require licenses, and if you take this work seriously and learn how to regularly generate assignments for yourself, you will make far more on an annual basis than the license costs. Besides, in most cases it is tax-deductible (check with your tax advisor)!

Melanie R. Jordan

Chapter Eight: Notes/Questions

Chapter Nine: Common Types of Shops, Are They Worth Your Time?

I am constantly amazed by the wide variety of shops that companies request to have done. Just when I think I have seen it all, I hear of a new one that surprises me. My recent favorites were for a maternity clothing store where you did not have to be pregnant (say you "just found out you were expecting", the guidelines said), and one for a tractor trailer driving school to check out the instruction.

Here are ten varieties of frequently-requested shops. I have included a summary of what is involved; what to ask before you accept; how much they tend to pay; if they are worth your time; and time management tips.

1. Apartment Shops (office space and home builder shops are similar)

What Is It? This is a two-step evaluation where you are asked to contact the apartment's leasing office by phone (phone shop), and then go visit the apartment complex and finish your evaluation on-site (on-site shop).

What's Involved? On the phone you are asked to pretend to look for an apartment and note among other things:

- how enthusiastic the leasing person is in helping you;

- how well they describe the facility or the apartment;

- how well they listen to your needs; and

- do they invite you in to tour the property.

On-site, you evaluate things such as if the employee:

- is professional in appearance;

- gives you a full tour of all the amenities and shows a vacant or model apartment;

- professionally handles your objections; and

- how hard they try to sell you on renting from them, or at least leaving a deposit.

Every company will have their own forms and ask you to emphasize some items over others. They may give you some additional instructions on the size of the apartment to ask for, how you should object when asked to rent, etc. But they are all pretty much the same, so once you have done a couple of them, they are very easy.

You will be asked to answer some easy "yes/no" questions (i.e. did the leasing agent do "X"?) and usually provide a few sentences on each aspect of your visit— phone and on-site, for a total of up to two written pages. Again, these detailed written sections are called narratives, and depending upon the type of shop, can be a few sentences or a few paragraphs. You must be able to write decently, although you do not have to win the Pulitzer!

<u>What to ask before you accept</u>—you need to know if the apartment shop is targeted or not. If there is a target, that

means there is a specific person that the mystery shopping company's client wants you to evaluate, and only a report based on your experience with that person is acceptable in order for you to be paid. If the shop is not targeted, this means that you can speak with any leasing agent and use them to do your entire evaluation.

Obviously an apartment shop without a target (sometimes called "random target") is preferable because it is easier. However, it may pay less so you have to weigh this versus the fact that a targeted shop will take more of your time. If the shop is a targeted one, you will also want to ask if the target's days off are supplied or if they know the best times to reach them (some mystery shopping companies will provide this information).

Plus, if a target is involved, know if you are permitted to ask for them on the phone (using a logical reason that does not tip off the fact that you are a shopper), or must you continue trying to reach them until they pick up the phone (making excuses to get off the line with other leasing agents who are not your target)? That makes a big difference.

Finally, be certain to know the rules as to how much time has gone by since you last did a shop at a particular location—common is 6 months.

Pay range: $20 to $50 ($25 to $30 is typical) depending upon your market and how desperate the company is to get the assignment completed.

<u>Worth Your Time</u>? Yes, if non-targeted or targeted but it's okay to ask for the person in a fashion that does not give away the shop. Targeted and "not allowed to ask for the person", with no other information such as days off, I would only take if I was short money for that month, it paid $30 or more, I was trying to break in with a new company, or gain more experience, because then the shop may take quite a bit more time as you work to reach the target. Of course, you could always reach them on the first or second try and then it really isn't an issue.

The more you do these shops, the faster you will perform them and write the reports, so they will become more and more worthwhile. Also, if you are a renter yourself, you can check out all the apartments in your area for future reference, or if you really are looking to make a change, and get paid to do it!

<u>Time Management Tips</u>—if you are assigned a targeted shop where you are not allowed to ask for the person, don't hesitate to ask the mystery shopping company for additional guidance or help in getting your specific target on the phone if you are having trouble getting hold of them. Each company will have their own definition in their guidelines of when to seek help—usually after 4-6 attempts.

I once had an apartment shop where I could not get hold of the target despite my best efforts, and I was not allowed to ask for the person (yes, I needed the money that time). When the mystery shopping company inquired with their client, it was discovered that this person was a bookkeeper for the property. She did conduct apartment tours, but it was very infrequent and she almost never answered the phone. We had to work together to conduct a scheme to get her to answer the phones for awhile— very challenging.

For any apartment shop assignment, do what you need to get the client the information they want, but no more. For example, if a leasing agent wants to show you multiple apartments, figure out a way to just see one of them. Seeing a second unit will not be necessary to properly do the shop and will just eat into your time.

Finally, make sure if it is a targeted shop, that the days the person you need to contact work match your availability and give you enough time to complete the assignment.

Tip: If you live in or near a major city and apartment guides are available, keep the latest versions of each one on hand. They are a handy reference on the property you will be visiting, so you can create a good shopper scenario by knowing the size of apartment, the price range and the amenities provided. Plus, the good leasing people will remember to ask how you heard of their property, so this way you can say "I saw your ad in For Rent Magazine" without missing a beat. These publications are free and readily available in your local supermarket or convenience store. You may also be able to access the information you need on-line.

2. <u>Fitness Center (Gym) Shops</u> (also bank shops, public storage facility and other service business shops are similar)

<u>What Is It</u>? This is usually a two-step evaluation where you are asked to contact the fitness center by phone (phone shop), and then go visit the center and finish your evaluation at the location (on-site shop). Note that a workout is usually not required (if it is the shop pays more).

<u>What's Involved</u>? You are asked to call and pretend that you are interested in joining the gym and observe among other things:

- how knowledgeable and enthusiastic the employee is;

- whether they describe the facility in detail or just immediately invite you in to tour the facility;

- if they ask about your fitness goals; and

- which membership plans they talk about.

On-site, you are asked to note items including:

- if the salesperson is well-groomed;

- if you are given a full tour of the club;

- which memberships were presented to you and the prices quoted;

- how they handled your objections to joining; and

- how hard they try to sell you on joining (note—you usually do not have to join as part of the assignment).

Every company will have their own forms and ask you to note some items in particular while offering additional guidelines. They are very easy and mostly consist of "yes/no" questions (i.e. did the sales rep do "X"?), and ask you for a few sentences only on your visit. The narrative is not lengthy at all.

What To Ask Before You Accept—nothing special here. Just make sure you know the rules as to how much time has gone by since you last did a shop at a particular location—common is 6 months to a year.

Pay Range: $15 - $40 (I have seen the upper end of this range when a company was desperate to get the shop done, or for a more elaborate scenario that required you to actually sign up and then cancel within the allotted time the local law allowed you for changing your mind. The lower end of the range is usually paid when you don't have to do the phone call part of the shop first, so there is a little less work involved).

Worth Your Time? Yes, this is an easy and usually very enjoyable shop. Plus, since the sales reps are supposed to be knowledgeable about fitness themselves and will often introduce you to a personal trainer as part of the tour, you can sneak in some questions you have about your own workouts or diet to test their knowledge and get free advice!

Time Management—most sales reps are usually pretty laid back and will try to sell (close) you only a time or two and then give up. Sometimes you may get a super salesperson who won't take no for an answer and try to get another person or two involved in selling you. It is important to note that they tried this for the shop and allow the other person to try and sell you for a moment or two so you do a good job for the client, but you do not have to subject yourself to endless selling pressure. Feel free to come up with an excuse to say you have to leave now but will be back tomorrow (i.e., "I am sorry, but I have to pick my child up at school").

3. Car Dealer Shops (also boat and RV shops are similar and you don't have to have much product knowledge)

What Is It? You will be asked to go to a car dealership and pretend you are interested in buying a car and test drive it (so you must be a licensed driver). No phone shop required; on-site only.

What's Involved? Simply show up at the assigned car dealership and make observations about the sales process. You will be asked to note things like:

- how long it took for a salesperson to approach you;

- what cars were recommended to you;

- what happened on the test drive;

- how the salesperson overcame your objections; and

- what the salesperson did to try to get you to buy a car that day.

The report forms will likely consist of some "yes/no" easy check-off answers, perhaps a brief question or two that requires a couple of sentences and a few paragraphs (about a page) describing the details of your visit.

<u>What To Ask Before You Accept</u>—nothing special here. Just be sure it is a dealer you don't mind going to, and that you are capable of completing the test drive. For example, if it is for a Jeep® dealership and you don't like driving big vehicles, don't volunteer for a shop for that dealership.

<u>Pay Range</u>: $25 - $30

<u>Worth Your Time</u>? Yes, if you learn how to manage the dealer's salespeople so you do not end up there all day. Plus, it is a lot of fun to be able to drive anything you want and get paid for it. I was always curious about what it would be like to drive a pick-up truck, so I recently accepted a Dodge® shop, test drove a Dodge Dakota and got paid for it (of course I didn't tell the salesperson that I never drove a truck before).

Another plus is that you can do these shops usually every four to six months so you don't have to wait a long time to repeat the shop. So many people stop in at these dealerships, they won't remember you anyway. One time

I had the same sales rep I had five months earlier for a shop at the dealership, and he did not have a clue that he had helped me before.

Time Management—this is one where you absolutely must keep the salesperson under control or you could be there for a couple of hours easily as I was when I first started doing these and didn't know any better. The most important thing to do is to communicate that your time is limited when they invite you back to the office to "work up some numbers".

Do not let them actually appraise your car (your client will likely just want to know if they offer to do so) as this takes a long time. Let them try to sell you a car to fulfill your client's needs, but tell them something like "if it will really only take a few minutes, as I have an appointment to get to at 3:00". If they keep you waiting for more than 10 minutes, start to walk around with your car keys in your hand showing your impatience.

After they have made a couple of attempts to close you (which is what you need to do for your client), be sure to say that you like the car very much, but you want to think about it overnight and you really do need to get going for your appointment. Remember, do what the client requires for your shop, but no more. I have gotten these car dealership shops down to about 45 minutes including the fun part of the test drive which is the amount of time they should take to make sense for you.

4. Oil Change Shops (car repair, carpet cleaning and testing centers are similar)

<u>What Is It</u>? Call to make an appointment for an oil change and then bring your car in for an actual oil change service. The phone shop is extremely brief and time spent on-site is the typical amount it takes to get your oil changed.

<u>What's Involved</u>? After setting your appointment up, bring in your car and make observations about how long it took; how helpful the service rep was; and what the waiting room was like. You will have some short "yes/no" questions and will need a couple of paragraphs (narrative) on your visit.

<u>What To Ask Before You Accept</u>: Verify if the shop just pays for the oil change or also includes payment for your time and doing the report.

<u>Pay Range</u>: $25 *plus* the cost of the oil change is typical. In my area, an oil change at the dealership is $24.77 including tax. So I earn $49.77 in cash and "merchandise" for this shop whenever I do it.

<u>Worth Your Time</u>? Yes, if one is available in your area, grab it! This is an extremely easy shop for something you do (or should do) for your car anyway. It takes about 5 minutes on the phone and 5 minutes to check in at the dealership. The next 45 minutes you'll be paid to sit in the waiting room to read a magazine or watch television! Your final 5 minutes of the shop will be to pay the cashier and get your car. A total of 1 hour. The report should take you a half hour maximum to complete.

As I mentioned, the company I work with not only covers the cost of the oil change, but also pays you for the shop. So you save on your budget *and* make money! If you figure your shop plus report time is an hour and a half, your hourly rate for this one is $33.18! Plus, there are no annoying sales pitches you have to subject yourself to (except maybe the typical "suggested maintenance items" they always seem to find), and you don't have to even do any pretending for this shop since you really are coming in for an oil change.

Time Management—tell them you need the car for a specific time (if at all possible) and you will wait for it. This keeps them from taking too long in servicing your car.

Tip—you can do multiple shops for different vehicles in the same time period. If you are a two or three car family, why not do this shop for each of your cars (if they are at different dealerships)? In fact, you can offer to take in your relatives' or friends' cars—they get the free oil change, you get paid $25 to take it in. Now that's what I call a win-win situation!

5. Retail Shops (clothing, department store, book store, sporting goods, linen, specialty store, factory outlet, party goods, video store, office supply store, wireless service, etc.—you name it, and a shop for it exists)

What Is It? You will be asked to pretend you are a typical customer of the store and make observations about the store's employees at the register and on the sales floor (where applicable). You may need to try something on in the case of a clothing store, so you need to be the appropriate size for that store's merchandise. A purchase may or may not be required. The reports are usually fast "yes/no" with a sentence or two here and there; no lengthy narratives

What's Involved? You will need to make note of:

- salesperson and cashier names and descriptions;

- your in-store experience or observe those of other customers;

- how the store is kept;

- how long you had to wait to get help or check out;

- whether the dressing rooms and rest rooms are clean (where applicable);

- how employees handle returns;

- did the employees try to increase the sale through up-selling (i.e. suggesting an item to go with what you would purchase);

In the case of an office supply or wireless store, you may be asked to test the floorperson's or salesperson's product/service and competitor knowledge and if they tried to sell you on something.

What to ask before you accept—find out if a purchase is required or not and if the item may be kept (with reimbursement made by the shopping company) or not. In many instances like I mentioned earlier when I shopped a bookstore, you got paid for the shop plus reimbursed for the cost of the book. If a purchase is required and you must return the item, (known as a "purchase and return shop") know whether the return can be made within an hour or two, or if you must come back another day.

<u>Pay Range</u>: $7- $25 plus possible reimbursement of up to $10 for a purchase.

<u>Worth Your Time</u>? It depends. If the shop is for a retail location that is right by your home, a place you shop anyway, your other job (if you have one), or a place you go to all the time anyway (like a gym, school, or day care center) it may be worth it to pick up a few extra bucks. Plus, getting an item free plus the shop fee, can make it all worthwhile. I personally try to get at least $15 cash and/or merchandise for any retail shop ($20 - $25 preferred).

If it is a purchase and return shop that leaves you with nothing to do for a couple of hours, or makes you come back another day, this should be at the upper end of the pay range, and located only in a place where your life would take you anyway. It's not worth your time or the gas expense to make more than one trip to a destination that is out of your way. You also are usually allowed to do these shops once a month or every other month, so you do not have to sit out for a long time period.

<u>Time Management</u>—These shops also frequently come up in malls besides local strip centers or freestanding

stores, so if you can make one trip to your local mall and do a couple of shops together, it can make lower-paying ones worth the effort. Remember, retailers tend to be spread out, so you need to plan your routes and try and complete shops in a logical travel pattern to save time and gas.

7. Fast Food Shops

What Is It? You'll be asked to make a purchase at a fast food chain restaurant, paying close attention to details. A reimbursable purchase will be required, and often a watch with a second-hand so you can time activities for the client. Keep in mind any dietary restrictions you may have as you also need to at least sample the food you order.

What's Involved? Your mission will be to order food at a fast food franchise where selections to be purchased may or may not be pre-determined by the client. You will need to make detailed observations of the employees so you can:

- give names and descriptions;

- note the timing of how long you waited in line and how long it took for your order to arrive;

- remember what was said to you;

- tell how many people were in line;

- describe the appearance of your food/was your order correct; and

- evaluate the cleanliness of the place and restrooms (if applicable).

The forms will probably be simple "yes/no" types with minimal narrative about the experience required.

<u>What To Ask Before You Accept</u>—Find out if you can order whatever you like from the menu (up to a certain amount) or if you must order meal combo #2 exactly. If you have to order something you don't even like, there is not much point to this shop! Also know whether you are simply going to be getting free food, or if you will paid at least something for your time. You also might be offered a compromise like $10 maximum reimbursement, and being allowed to keep what you don't spend after a reasonable purchase that meets the shop requirements is made.

<u>Pay Range</u>: $5 - $15 either in free food, food + shop fee or reimbursement + keeping whatever is left over.

<u>Worth Your Time</u>? Maybe. I did some of these in the beginning just to get experience and break in with new companies. Today, I would not do them for less than the top end of the range ($15), and, of course, it must be a local place that I actually want to go to. It is also preferable if it is a regular assignment.

<u>Tip</u>: Combine one of these fast food shops with a retail shop in your local mall or strip shopping center, or an

apartment shop (take yourself out to lunch) for an assignment that becomes worthwhile overall.

8. Restaurant Shops

<u>What Is It</u>? You'll get to dine with a companion at anything from a casual dining chain restaurant to an upscale local restaurant. You will also probably have more latitude in what you order with guidelines usually indicating whether or not you need to order a drink, an appetizer, an entrée and dessert.

<u>What Is Involved</u>: Simply put—having lunch or dinner (sometimes breakfast) and making very detailed observations similar to a fast food shop, but you'll be there longer, eat more food and interact with and observe more employees and other customers' experiences. Be prepared for a hefty amount of narrative, and if you are shopping a more upscale restaurant, you must dress up and look and act the part.

<u>What To Ask Before You Accept</u>—Similar to a fast food shop you need to know what you must order and if it is compatible with your tastes or lifestyle. Don't accept a shop that involves drinking alcohol (unless someone else you are dining with can handle this for you) if you don't like to drink. Or if you follow an "NMP" eating style like I do (no meat or poultry—if you are interested in finding out more about my unique approach to healthy eating and living, check out my other book *Have Your Cheeseburger And Keep Your Health Too!* on my web site Healthy Eating Coach's Corner at www.healthyeatingcoach.com), don't volunteer for a steakhouse assignment. Know the

payment structure as well—are you just getting reimbursed, or are you getting at least a token shop fee too?

<u>Pay Range</u>: Depends on the restaurant (major cities pay more because the dinner costs more), but usually covers a nice dinner for two including all aspects from drinks to dessert, gratuity and parking (if valet). Figure a range of $35 to $100. Additional shop fees, if offered, are a token amount of $10 or less.

<u>Worth Your Time</u>? Yes. This is one of those situations where you will earn an item that stretches your budget if you normally do go out, or lets you have a night out that you might not otherwise have. You are being paid to socialize with a friend, family member or loved one with free food. Another benefit is that someone else is along to help you make mental notes so you can better remember details for your report. You can also easily fit this into your schedule as a second shop on some days and eat out one or two nights a week for free!

When you consider that you could be getting $35 - $100 in free dining and drinks, you can see how these shops combined with your non-food shops could easily get you in the $1,000 in a month earnings category. I love getting to eat out regularly at my favorite restaurants or try new ones with someone else footing the bill!

<u>Tip</u>: Know that the amount you receive as the reimbursement for your meal is generally considered taxable since it is your pay—please check with your tax advisor.

9. Web Site & Phone Shops

<u>What Is It</u>? Just like companies want to know about how their physical locations and the employees that run them measure up, they also want to see how their web sites and call centers are perceived. Sometimes, they might want to just know how their people are on the phone even when there is a physical business location. Some shops are a combination of using a web site and calling a central customer service phone number to see how these folks handle an inquiry.

<u>What's Involved</u>? You'll be asked to evaluate a web site by trying it out and seeing if:

- it is well laid out;

- easy to use;

- if all the links worked;

- if everything loaded; and

- overall, how easy was it for you to get the information you needed?

You will likely be asked to contact customer service via e-mail (or possibly by phone) and note their response(s) and how long it took.

For a customer call center, you might be asked to:

- inquire about an item;

- attempt to place an order (or place one and send the item back noting how the order and return were handled);

- note how long it took for someone to answer your call/ how long you were on hold; and

- were the phone representatives polite and knowledgeable?

What To Ask Before You Accept—Find out if you need to order anything or just make an inquiry. Be sure you will be reimbursed for shipping and postage if you have a mail order purchase and return. Determine if you are being paid by the call or a flat fee for the project and make sure you are being compensated enough for what is asked of you. See how much narrative (if any) is required.

Pay Range: $10 to $20 + applicable reimbursement for postage/shipping; as high as $50 for a web site/phone combination.

Worth Your Time? Yes for web site evaluations (I did one recently for an automotive dealership and got paid $20 for about 20 minutes worth of work and did not have to leave my house. Talk about being able to fit work into your schedule! I did this at 10:30 at night.

Yes also for phone work—again as long as the phone calls are toll-free or local and the pay is at least $15 for no more than an hour's work. Again, you don't have to leave the house so you save gas and travel time. If you have to do a very elaborate scenario with buying something, sending it back, etc., it's probably not worth it. If you see web or phone shops grab them!

Tip: There's a site that is working with both U.S. and Canadian mystery shoppers that is exclusively devoted to web site mystery shopping. To find out more about Web Mystery Shoppers and sign up to work with them, check out www.webmysteryshoppers.com. They even pay a referral fee if you recommend a business web site that hires their company to do a web-based shop.

10. Video And Audio Mystery Shops

<u>What Is It</u>? Basically, you are conducting a shop just as you would one that does not involved the use of equipment, but you are either using a hidden audio or video recorder to capture every aspect of your shop. Please note that this is a type of shop that I recommend for you once you are a more experienced shopper, rather than a newbie or beginner. I believe you should be comfortable first with conducting several shops before you add the complexities of carrying hidden equipment. I have a full chapter on this in my other *book How-To Finally Make Money As A Mystery Shopper* called *Video Mystery Shopping* which I recommend that you read as soon as you have a few good shops under your belt, if you did not already receive it as part of purchasing my *Mystery Shopping 2-Volume Set*. It's available for purchase 24/7 at http://www.mysteryshoppercoach.com/books.html.

<u>What To Ask Before You Accept</u>—Find out if the company supplies and maintains the equipment you will be using

during your shop, or if you must purchase your own. I have found that most companies expect you to have the micro-sized audio recorder, but many do lend out the video equipment (it's not the same kind you use on vacation or to take pictures of your kids). I suggest you take on video shops only where they will provide you with the equipment until you are sure you want to do this kind of work on an ongoing basis.

Pay Range: $20 to $50 for audio shops; $20 to $100 for video shops.

Worth Your Time? In most cases, yes. Although I would suggest that you look for $30 or more for any shop that involved the use of equipment. A major plus is that video shops usually do not have any additional paper report to complete post-shop, as your video is your report. However, this can be a drawback if you have technical difficulties and your report does not record properly, is damaged or accidentally gets erased.

Keep in mind, there are lots of other types of shops I have not gone into detail about and new ones pop up all the time—haircuts, hotels, movie theaters, grocery stores, carpet cleaning, gas stations, testing centers, retirement homes, day care centers, etc.

The shops I have previously-discussed should give you a good idea of what is generally involved on any assignment and whether it is worth your time or not. Consider these factors, plus whether the shop is for something you need (i.e. if you were about to get a haircut anyway and you like the salon or store where you would have to go). In this case, it may make sense for you to do the assignment even if you are only getting reimbursed for your haircut and not getting paid extra for actually doing the shop. You still got a free haircut that stretches your budget because it did not have to come out of your own pocket!

Also consider whether the shop is to do something you like doing. If going to evaluate a day care center is not something you want to do, even if you do have a child available to you, don't do it. Finally, be sure to factor in your time, gas expense and wear and tear on your vehicle in going to a shop to be sure it makes sense for you.

Chapter Nine: Notes/Questions

Chapter Ten: Okay, I'm In. How Do I Get Started?

Many books that have been published on mystery shopping advise you to apply to any and all mystery shopping companies left and right. I recently saw someone proudly post on a message board that she had applied to over 200 companies and got a shop assignment. If I spent my time applying to 200 companies, I wouldn't be so thrilled that I got "a" shop. I disagree with the "apply to hundreds of companies" approach.

Some people give me a lot of heat over this point, but I know the ways that I advise shoppers to secure their assignments *really* work. There are those that say "nonsense—apply, apply, apply", but I am sorry, they are not working efficiently or smartly. Besides, who are you going to believe—an anonymous post on a discussion board from someone who is probably making $100 a month, or a professional mystery shopping expert like me who's done it?

One reason I don't believe in the "mass application approach" is because many of these companies give preference to shoppers with at least some experience. In addition, the odds of a particular company having an assignment in your area, and then bothering to go through their database to find you is slim. The larger, and many of the better, mystery shopping companies outsource the booking of their mystery shopping jobs with people known as schedulers. This makes sense. Why should a company bother trying to find a shopper for a particular assignment—especially on short notice—when they can pass along whole batches of jobs ordered by their clients to the independent agents who handle that aspect of things for them?

And even when they do handle assignment bookings in-house, it's better to apply in response to actual job leads they post in one of many places on the internet. Think of a "real world" job search. If you just apply to companies all over the place without any experience, or knowing if they even have any job openings, it's going to be a fruitless effort. Plus, once you are awarded an assignment applied for in this fashion, you are in the company's database as a proven shopper who they are familiar with—quite a difference!

Keep in mind that you want to spend your time actually doing assignments (where you earn money) and not spend your time searching for, and trying to land assignments (where you do not earn money). Time spent looking for work is time spent not working…and making money!

If you follow my instructions, you'll make the right connections and have jobs coming to you all the time (assuming you do a good job as a shopper of course), rather than you having to search for them or check assignments on tons of web sites you've randomly applied to (not good use of your time). Today, mystery shopping is a matter of getting known by those who control the big batches of jobs. These are the middlemen, (or should I say "middlewomen" since just about all I have come across are female) I referred to earlier known as schedulers. There are independent schedulers who handle the assignments of many different mystery shopping companies, and company schedulers, who just handle just the jobs of the company for which they work.

Generally, it is much better use of your time to get known by several independent schedulers who will be handling multiple assignments for all different companies on an ongoing basis, than having to find a job here from company A and a job there from company B. Company schedulers who are also aggressive enough to post job openings on lead boards and through other resources are also worth knowing. Trust me, this is the fastest way to get your shopping jobs and more importantly, <u>keep getting shopping assignments coming to you</u>! Please note that you don't have to pay anything to schedulers, they are compensated by the mystery shopping company for matching you up with one of their assignments.

So how do you reach the schedulers? They regularly post job leads to one of several shopper message boards that are updated on the internet—sometimes many times a day as new job leads come in. I will also let you in on a secret—most of the schedulers seem to post to all of the major lead boards which means you do not have to review every single one that exists for fear of missing out on an assignment opportunity. You can check out any of the following and decide which two or three serve your needs best.

If you are one of my readers from Canada or another country outside the United States, I will note which sources will apply specifically to you. By going onto a country-specific version of Yahoo, like Yahoo Canada, you can likely turn up other lead boards and groups not mentioned here.

Some of my favorites are Yahoo Groups. These are all discussion groups catering to those looking for leads for mystery shopping assignments and to connect with schedulers. Most of them require that you be approved to join the group. Not a big deal really, just follow the instructions and you'll be added—they just want to avoid spammers or those who aren't really interested in the topic at hand that will cause trouble.

Simply go to the main Yahoo Groups page at: http://groups.yahoo.com. Then type in the name(s) of the group(s) you wish to join, one by one. Here are several top ones:

- mysteryshoppingbyncpms
- mystery-shopper
- mystery-shops
- mysteryshopspay45
- mystery_shoppers_usa
- restaurantbarms
- secret-shopper
- lots-o-funms

This will bring you to each group's main page where you can click on "join this group" and be added instantly, or after being approved.

Depending on the volume of messages, or how often you tend to see listings in your area in their postings, you can either select individual delivery of e-mails to get access to postings fastest (but you will have a bunch of e-mails in your in-box, or adjust the setting for e-mail delivery to digest form for very active group (downside is you may miss out on assignments when you only get one e-mail a day). If you don't mind having a bunch of e-mails, you can quickly scan the headings to see what isn't appropriate and hit "delete" as you read subject lines that clearly you have no interest in.

In the future, you won't have to check these resources as often because you'll be known and in all the key company and individual schedulers databases. It will also give you a good idea in the beginning of the various kinds of shops that come up, and what they tend to pay and require so you can decide what you want to try for.

If you subscribe to Delphi newsgroups (similar to Yahoo Groups) there are several devoted to mystery shopping. Just go to www.delphiforums.com and enter the topic "mystery shopping" to get a list of newsgroups that are available. Some are geared to a particular state, some to just offering leads, and others to offering information and assistance. Canadian shoppers—there is a Delphi group just for you located at http://forums.delphiforums.com/canshoppers/start. Check through the various offerings and see if any of them are of interest to you. But pick a couple of favorites and that's it!

Topica has a very good mailing list as well at: http://www.topica.com/lists/msopenings

The Mystery Shoppers Providers Association (MSPA), a trade association for businesses who offer mystery shopping services also has a section that sometimes has leads for shoppers—both in the U.S., as well as Canada, Europe and other countries. Go to www.mysteryshop.org/shoppers, you'll be taken to a page where you can sort your search by your location, type of assignment you are looking for, etc. There is also a board for networking with other mystery shoppers. By the way, don't worry about the certifications they talk about—you don't need them!

In addition to working with the resources I have listed above, You'll want to get into the shopper databases of the two largest scheduling companies—Kern Scheduling Services and Palm Scheduling Services. Some changes have occurred recently with both of these companies that is important to understand in working with them. Kern and Palm have transitioned many of their jobs over to automated systems that have pros and cons for mystery shoppers. On the plus side, if you are in the overall database for each of these companies, you'll theoretically be "known" to each of their schedulers when the system sends out e-mails for their job assignments without worrying that you've missed somebody. Plus, when you want to take the initiative and look for jobs on your own for some reason (remember your goal is to spend as little time looking for work as possible—let the leads come to you), or if you are traveling (see Chapter Nine for more on this), you can see what's doing in a particular area.

On the negative side, these automated systems take some of the personal contact out of your interaction with a mystery shopping company and/or scheduler, so it's harder to get known and not just be one person in a sea of mystery shoppers. These new systems also tend to provide rankings of shoppers through a formula so higher-ranked shoppers get preference for an assignment (this can be a pro or a con depending how you are ranked and what goes into the rating system).

Be very careful with these automated systems to put down all applicable areas to be sure you are not left out of any prime assignments that happen to be on the border of your city or share an area code.

To get into the Kern Scheduling Services database, go to: http://www.kernscheduling.com.

To get into the Palm Scheduling Services database, go to: www.palmschedulingservices.com.

There are also many sites which I call "pay for leads" sites that offer shoppers the opportunity to register for an annual fee or lifetime fee, and then provide any or all of the following services: they deliver shop assignment leads to you by e-mail from the schedulers who post jobs to their sites; let companies and schedulers find you via a profile; and allow you to search for shops on their site.

I've personally put two of these services to the test and generally find they could be of value for some shoppers—especially if you combine the methods for marketing yourself to schedulers in this book with the additional lead contacts you'll make through these services. Yet, you also need to be careful, as there are certainly many other sites out there which are requiring payment that are nothing but scams. Overall, do not in any way feel that it is necessary to sign up for a "pay for leads" site, as you can certainly get by without signing up for these services since you are already empowered by the knowledge in this book.

Tip: *If you haven't already thought of this, consider adding a free e-mail address account such as those available from Yahoo for your newsgroup or newsletter correspondence. Not for your schedulers and company contacts, since you want those going to your primary, professional e-mail address. Use this secondary freebie e-mail address to subscribe to newsgroups or newsletters so you can read these at your leisure. Plus if you sign-up for several, they will not clutter up your main e-mail address where those money-generating e-mail messages are coming in. If you find a newsgroup is turning into a great source of leads for you and they have a subscribe option, you can always change the e-mail address that their messages are delivered to over to your primary address.*

Overall, you'll find that using two or three favorites as your primary lead resources may be all you need to get started. In the beginning though, you'll likely want to check several leads resources to make sure you have your bases covered and until you see which ones are the best fits for you. You also may need to do more searching among the resources like the MSPA to find shops if you live in a less-populated area.

Once you make contact with several schedulers, they will add you to their databases as an active shopper in your area, and e-mail you job leads for their assignments usually before, or at least simultaneously, with postings on the job lead boards. Sometimes, schedulers will even call you or e-mail you personally to ask you if you would like a particular job once you get well-known by them and have proven yourself. I was fortunate to get into this category. As a reader of this book, you too will be soon!

This is another reason why you don't need to get obsessed with reviewing dozens of lead boards or applying to hundreds of companies. Now while I believe connecting with schedulers is optimal for the reasons I have given, I know shoppers get antsy about networking, or do not always have timely e-mail access to jump on the latest shopper opportunities that the schedulers they are connected with send their way. Also many shoppers like to do jobs when they travel, and want easy access to assignments in the area to which they will be heading.

So now I'll share with you a secret. **There is one type of company, and only one that makes sense to apply to directly, as you have some spare time. To learn the secret of the only mystery shopping web sites you should ever apply to directly, go to http://www.mysteryshoppercoach.com/secretsites.html**

Chapter Ten: Notes/Questions

Chapter Eleven: Reviewing Listings And Getting Your First Assignment

When you get your e-mail updates or if you locate a lead that sounds good from one of the board resources), review them right away. The most desirable assignments go fast! To save time, just scan the headings for your state or any that say "shoppers needed in many states". If you live in California, you are not doing a shop in South Carolina tomorrow in all likelihood, so don't bother reading about the assignment.

As you see an assignment that is in your area, read the message carefully to see what specific cities jobs are in, details about the assignment like pay, due date, what is required, and most importantly, how to respond. Be sure you do what the scheduler asks to have the best shot of getting the job or to at least be considered for future jobs.

If they say to e-mail them with the city of the job in the heading, do it. If they say call, do it. If they ask you to supply certain information about yourself, do it. If they tell you they are posting for a friend and you must e-mail their friend and not them, absolutely do it. The ability to follow instructions is an important part of being a good shopper—demonstrate this by following them in applying for the assignment. If you can't follow instructions to get the job, why should you get the job?

You have two goals in responding to job leads posted by the schedulers:

- To get the job you are applying for; and

- To get in their database for direct e-mail notification of future assignments

So how do you get that elusive first assignment under your belt? I found you just had to be persistent and keep answering lead board postings and the job assignments started happening. I had my first assignment within the first couple of days. At first I took anything, because I wanted to say I had experience with several different companies to establish credibility and to cover different types of shops. This showed I could handle just about anything. Plus, if you are good enough to be working with several different companies, you must be doing something right, so other schedulers will also tend to give you assignments. Then the snowball effect begins.

Remember, no one ever checks how long you have worked as a shopper or calls a former employer. Your first assignment will likely be secured by a scheduler needing emergency help because another shopper cancelled. This is your foot in the door; it certainly was mine.

I think it is a good idea to get experience in retail, restaurant or fast food and service categories (automotive, apartments, banking, fitness centers for example). It shows diversity and that you can handle all types of observations—quick checklists and lengthy narratives. It is also good to try and get "in" with a major mystery shopping company by taking any initial assignment. You can be more selective later on.

Again, your service category shops (and audio/video shops once you have some experience) will generally pay the most and demonstrate that you are a higher caliber shopper, so try to focus on them. If you are serious about earning as much as possible doing mystery shopping work, that's where the money is. Besides, you will also get your best chance of securing other work, like report editing, by showing what you can do on those narrative sections.

As I mentioned earlier in this chapter, since your goal is to get into as many schedulers' databases as possible, always have a statement in your e-mail response to an assignment posting saying if the assignment is not available, to please add you to their database for future assignments. Schedulers always need to know about new, available people and you will hear from them down the line.

In the Resource Section at the end of his book, I have included the response letter I use which I tweak to fit the particular job assignment I am going for. You should review it and then create one *in your own voice and style*. Essentially, you should have the following components in addition to any specifics the scheduler has asked for:

- put the city, state and type of shop in the subject section of your e-mail (unless other instructions for response are given).

- indicate the job you are contacting the scheduler about (type, city, state, due date) and how you heard about it.

- let me repeat this because it is so important—<u>have a line saying that if this assignment is no longer available, please add you to their database for future jobs</u>.

- mention any experience you have—some companies you regularly work with and types of shops <u>(do not ever name specific clients for these shops (i.e. Joe's gym)</u>. If you are new to mystery shopping, tell the scheduler something about yourself or your other work experiences that address what makes a good shopper. For myself, it was my prior marketing and market research experience and the fact that I was in retailing and financial services (since many shops are available in these industries).

- list when you are generally available to work and if your hours are flexible, if you are available weekdays, weekends or both, etc.

- include some of your qualities that make you (or would make you) a good shopper, such as your ability to meet deadlines, that you pay close attention to details, you are PC literate, etc.

- provide the cities/towns you will shop in (knowing that the distance is reasonable given your time and that you are not reimbursed for gas/mileage).

- thank the scheduler for their time and provide all your key contact information in a block of type— name, e-mail address, address, phone number and fax number or signature file if your e-mail program allows you to do so.

Now of course, if you are responding to an automated e-mail lead generated by a scheduling system, you won't have the chance to include these items, but there are enough companies and schedulers out there who are directly reviewing e-mails they get in response to assignments, so it pays to be able to write a good job lead response e-mail for those situations. You also may be able to sometimes include a little more information about yourself on certain forms—always look out for the chance to stand out from the crowd whenever you can.

Chapter Eleven: Notes/Questions

Chapter Twelve: You Got the Job! How To Be Sure You Do A Great Job So You Get Another Job!

Congratulations! Here are the nine steps to take you through the assignment process from receipt through report submission to ensure you do a great job every step of the way.

1. Create Your File for the Shop

Make a folder for each company that you are doing a shop for. Print out the confirmation e-mail sent by the scheduler or company, or if you got the assignment by phone, be sure to review the instructions sent. Often these e-mails will have forms, shopper guidelines and possibly payroll vouchers or invoice forms that you must eventually send in to get paid (many schedulers and companies will put you in for payment automatically when your completed report is sent in).

Download any files immediately and save them in a file on your computer where you can find them again (I also usually keep the e-mail in an Outlook folder as back-up until the job is completed). Also print out everything in these downloads—forms, guidelines, etc. for your file. These will be your records that prove you were assigned the shop. They also provide proof of the instructions you were given for completing the shop in case any conflicts arise. Plus, it is important to download files immediately to be sure that you do not have any problems doing so.

2. Read Through All the Materials

Look closely for deadlines, and how long you have after the shop to send in your final report. Here's the tricky part—even if the shop isn't due for three more days, the company may require you to send in the shop report within 24 hours or 48 hours after completion. Also be aware of payment information—you may need to submit an invoice to the company, how to submit the report and receipts, and if your scheduler wants to receive a copy of the final report (some do, some don't). Make notes as you read everything. Now is the time to ask any questions you have about the assignment.

If after you have thoroughly read all materials sent you have some questions, do not hesitate to call or e-mail the contact at the company that is given in your assignment. If you absolutely cannot get through to the company, ask the scheduler for assistance in getting the information you need to complete the job properly.

There is a reason why a research assignment is structured a certain way based on the clients' needs. If you do not do the assignment correctly, you have ruined the clients' research for that location; you have made the company and scheduler who hired you look bad, you will get penalized in your shopper payment or perhaps won't get paid at all and you will hurt your chances of getting future work from the company or the scheduler. So don't be afraid to ask questions to be sure you do the job the way the client wants the research done. And again, keep in mind that every client and mystery shopping company has their own methods of doing their field research. Just because one company handles it a particular way, do not assume all your shops will be exactly the same within the same category. I regularly did apartment shops for several companies, and each of their client property management companies does things a little differently.

3. Put Key Dates for the Assignment in Your Calendar

Once you know what is involved (is it a targeted shop, is a phone call and in-person visit required, etc.), and the deadline, note on your calendar (your planner, your electronic planner, etc.) the day(s) when you plan to do the assignment; when you will do the report; and one for when the job is due as a reminder. Don't forget to allow yourself time for all components of the shop and the completed report. Note also that when you want to do the shop, may not line up with when the company wants it done—see if they mention any days of the week or times of day to avoid.

4. Create Your Character/Story for the Shop

This should be fun for you. After you completely understand the assignment, using the guidelines you were given, create your "undercover" personality and story. If you know you are going to do a retail shop and you aren't familiar with that store, go on the internet and see if they have a web site that you can look at so you know what kinds of items they sell and prepare yourself. If you are going to a car dealer, make sure you know what kind of Dodge you want to "buy".

Have answers prepared for logical questions that the employees you are going to request assistance from as part of the shop would be likely to ask. If you are looking for an apartment, know why you are moving; when your lease is up; your budget; and what you are looking for in an apartment. If you are going to do be doing shops for a client that has many locations where you have to have a different identity for each (like a gym shop), write down and practice your name, address and phone number so they come out naturally when asked.

5. <u>Get Directions</u>

As part of the phone portion of your shop, you may be offered directions. Or it may be your job to wait and see if they offer any directions, and then ask for them if they don't and note it in your report. If neither one is the case, look up directions yourself on the web. One good spot is through <u>www.yahoo.com</u>. Click on the subheading that says "maps" and then on the link that says "get directions". Put in your location, and the shop location, and you will have door-to-door directions you can print out. It is also handy if you are going from one shop to another and don't know how to easily get from one site to the next. You'll save yourself time and gas!

6. <u>Conduct Your Shop</u>

Carefully follow the instructions and guidelines you were given. Be sure that when you conduct your shop, you get all the information you are supposed to report on. For a phone shop, have a piece of paper in front of you or an extra copy of the shop form with your alias and made-up contact phone number (if applicable), so it is handy. Note the time of your call (and when it finishes) as you are dialing on the same paper. Prompt yourself to listen for the number of rings; a particular greeting; and the name of the people you are dealing with by phone by putting a couple of blank lines on the same piece of paper in front of you that you fill in as you are talking. Take notes to help you fill in the questions and any required narratives later on.

Tip—*Don't use a pencil for taking notes, the sound can easily carry through the phone. Also, if you are making up a phone number and do not have your phone number blocked for caller ID services, see if your phone company lets you block your number on a per call basis so you don't give away your real number.*

For on-site shops, if you are driving, set your odometer to zero so can easily track your mileage for tax reporting purposes (or if you are lucky enough to be getting reimbursed for mileage). Be sure to take your directions and a blank copy of the shop forms with you, but leave the forms in your car or put them in your pocket or purse where they cannot be seen. Be aware of the time you arrived at the store or assigned location and when you left. Please note, you may have to do this mentally at the location—you usually can't take notes unless it is a retail shop (where you can or are maybe even required to stop in the bathroom to evaluate its cleanliness so you can jot a few notes mid-shop).

Be sure you are observing or asking what is necessary to gather the information you need later—especially employee names and descriptions (try saying the name and description in your head several times to memorize it—like Joey, brown hair, green eyes, no glasses, short hair, tall and slim). Once you drive or walk a bit away from the location you have shopped, you can pull out your shop report forms and make notes as quickly as possible so you will remember your experience in the greatest detail. Once you have your notes, names, descriptions and times down on paper, relax! You can do your full report later (unless it's a very simple check-off type form with no narrative—in which case you probably already finished it).

7. Reporting

Carefully fill out the shop forms and if possible, put any longer narratives on a separate Microsoft® Word (or a plain text) document and just state "see attached document for narrative details". I have found that most shopping companies' forms are not geared well towards the narrative portion. Review your forms for obvious grammatical errors, accuracy, misspellings (use your spell check) and potential conflicts between what you said in answering a question versus what is in your narrative. If you checked off "no" when asked if you would buy a car from this dealer, but later in the narrative say how well they treated you and the good deal they gave you, that would not make sense.

You should also make sure you just give factual answers and save any opinions or suggestions until the end of the report if asked for them. Remember, you are a researcher, and researchers report facts. Again, be sure that the report is being submitted within the allotted time after the shop has been completed even if the deadline is a few days away. For example, it's June 9th, your shop is due by June 12th and your report must be filed 24 hours after shop completion. You did the shop June 10th, which means your report is due June 11th even though your overall shop deadline gave you till June 12th.

If you will be e-mailing your report, be sure to follow any instructions about naming your saved file for the company's convenience.

8. Report Submission

Review the guidelines and any instructions from either the scheduler or mystery shopping company to be sure that you properly submit your report. An incomplete report may not be accepted, or your payment may be reduced. Include any requested documents such as receipts (very important for retail, airport or restaurant shops where you are going to be reimbursed), business cards, apartment floor plans, etc. Use the right method of submission and be certain that the method you choose does not result in a reduced fee if at all possible (i.e. faxing vs. e-mail can often result in a lower payment).

If you are e-mailing, make sure that you have attached your report as a file (it's easy to forget if you rush), and send the report to the e-mail address you have been instructed to use (not your scheduler unless they have specifically requested to receive a copy). Put something like "Joe's XYZ Shop, Anywhere, CA Complete" as the subject line and a short note (see the Resource Section for a sample).

Essentially you want to accomplish the following with this note:

- repeat which report is included;

- tell the company to please contact you if they have any questions or problem opening the attachment;

- state that you would appreciate confirmation that the report has been received; and

- indicate you enjoyed working with the company, appreciated the opportunity and hope to do so again soon.

Conclude your message by signing off with your contact information block/signature.

If your scheduler has not requested to receive a copy of your report submission, send him or her an e-mail letting them know that the report has been completed and sent to the contact at the e-mail address they instructed you to use. Also mention that you enjoyed working with them and hope to do so again soon. If this is the first time you are working with the particular scheduler, remind them to please include you in their database and e-mails of assignments they need help with. Sign off with your contact block/signature. (There is also a sample of this letter in the Resource Section for your convenience).

Taking the little bit of extra time to send e-mail correspondence like this is good business etiquette—much like when you write a thank you note for a job interview. Not everyone does it, and it helps you look professional and stand out in a positive way for future assignment consideration. You'd be surprised at how often your e-mail will arrive at just the moment when a rush job came in, or another shopper cancelled on that scheduler. Of course you, the professional mystery shopper who just took an extra moment to stand out from the crowd, got that job!

9. After You Have Submitted Your Shop

Print out a copy of your report, your cover e-mail or fax. Place that along with any receipts, business cards or other materials from the shop in your file for the company in case they did not get your report, or you need back-up materials to help with questions from the mystery shopping company or client later on. Keep these items until you are paid for the shop (and the check clears if it is the first time you have worked with a particular company). Then you can throw out the report if you like. I usually save at least a sample of a report for each type of shop I do for future reference.

Next, you should log the shop information into your records so you will know about payment due dates; and can keep track of how much you are earning for the month and when you can do the shop again (if there are restrictions). E-mail me at Melanie@mysteryshoppercoach.com for a free copy of my cool Excel spreadsheet that tracks all of the necessary information along with a running total of your monthly earnings.

If the company you are working with requires you to send an invoice or some other type of payroll form at the end of the month for all the shops you have completed for them (fill in the form as you go during the month to save time and so you don't forget any shops), put a note on your calendar to remind you to send it in so you get paid promptly.

I also recommend putting a note in your calendar as to when you should receive your payment by based on their stated guidelines. If a week past that date goes by without your receiving a payment, drop a polite e-mail, or make a polite phone call, to the mystery shopping company's office (not your scheduler), to verify the status—sometimes records fall through the cracks. When you receive the payment, make a note in your records or on my information sheet.

Chapter Twelve: Notes/Questions

Chapter Thirteen: What To Do When You Do Apply To Companies Individually

If you do all of the following, you will have plenty of schedulers and mystery shopping companies contacting you for assignments, so you may never need to apply to company web sites individually:

- keep answering job leads from the boards, or mailing lists;

- act like a professional;

- get your assignments done on time;

- do them well; and

- hand in quality reports.

However, for those of you who are antsy, as a secondary step, you can also register with companies directly. Again, I would use this as an extra step as you have a few minutes here and there—your priority should be on answering job board leads sent to you and getting on schedulers' databases/e-mail lists. Plus, I would wait until you have at least worked at some mystery assignments— even a couple will do—so you can answer the question "do you have mystery shopping experience" with a "yes".

There are hundreds of companies out there and if you apply to all of them, the vast majority will be a total waste of your time for the reasons I discussed in the previous chapter. **There is only one time you should apply**

directly to a company! To learn the secret, go to: http://www.mysteryshoppercoach.com/secretsites.ht ml

When you do apply to these special sites, on their individual web pages, wherever it says "become a shopper", "register as a shopper", "shoppers", etc., fill out the on-line form and you're registered.

Most companies will ask for the basics:

- your contact information (name, address, phone, fax, e-mail);

- demographic questions like age, race, sex; your social security number (do this only on secure web pages);

- do you own a car and what type;

- do you have a major credit card (to determine if it will be easy for you to perform retail shops—don't give out your credit card number);

- the days/times you are available for shops;

- do you mind shops involving alcohol or tobacco products; and

- what cities/towns you would be willing to shop in without being reimbursed for mileage (note if this is a sizable list, have the cities saved in a Word document that you can then cut and paste onto the form).

Tip: Your browser should indicate when you are on a secure web page. If it is not secure, e-mail the company and ask for an alternative method of delivering that piece of information. For security reasons, never e-mail your social security number!

Many shoppers ask me about giving out their social security number even on a secure site to a company they do not know. I advise that if you have doubts, don't input your real number. Either note in the form's comments section "social security number to be supplied on receipt of first assignment"; or contact the company directly and explain the situation. In a pinch, if the form won't go through without a number in the social security field, input all 9's and correct it when you actually start working with the company.

Then some mystery shopping company web sites will require a little more of you. They want to see how you write and think and will ask you questions like:

- Why do you want to be a mystery shopper?

- Why do companies use mystery shoppers?

- What would you do if someone asked if you were a shopper?

- Describe your best customer service experience.

- Describe your worst customer service experience.

In the Resource Section, I have sample responses to each of these questions. Read them *and change them so they are in your voice and style.* Add this to the Word document that has your cities list so that you can just open up this document. I have mine labeled "shopper response examples" and cut and paste this information to the company's form.

Tip: On some sites, you can't just use edit cut and edit paste, you have to use the control key (ctrl) on your computer plus the "c" key to copy and ctrl plus the "v" key to paste the information on the form.

There may also be a section on the web site application that gives you the freedom to provide additional information. Use it to include some of your experience and qualities that make you a great shopper "find" for that company.

For your records, you should keep the following information easily accessible:

- a list of companies you have applied to;

- each company's web site address;

- the date you applied;

- password or user name that you created or were assigned from the company for future access;

- whether or not the company posts their job leads on their web site;

- how often leads are updated; and

- does the company e-mail you when a local assignment is available?

I'll be happy to e-mail you a free, handy form I have set up just for this purpose if you contact me at Melanie@mysteryshoppercoach.com.

Personally, unless it is a company I regularly do work with (and in those cases, they are almost always contacting me first anyway), I tend to just keep up with the companies that will e-mail me when they have an assignment in my area with the specific job in the message, or at minimum, a notification that new assignments in my area are posted on their web site to check out. Also be aware that some web sites are sophisticated enough to contact you with jobs that really are in your area, while others will contact you if it is anywhere in your state.

When I was doing my mystery shopping work full-time, I lived in California, a very big state. It was annoying and a waste of time to get an e-mail for an assignment that was 600 miles away. But that's the price you pay for also knowing that there is a job you are interested in just five miles away.

Chapter Thirteen: Notes/Questions

Chapter Fourteen: How To Maximize Your Income As A Mystery Shopper By Standing Out From The Crowd (For Anyone—New Or Experienced)

Based upon my experience, here are 10 ways that you can earn the most from your mystery shopping work whether you are brand new or have some experience.

1. Be a Professional

The first thing you should do after you have your professional working environment set up as we discussed earlier (including your proper voicemail greeting), is to create some sample e-mail correspondence that can be used in your dealings with schedulers. They should consist of:

- Sample Response to a Job Lead Posting

- "Keep Me in Mind" Response (for when you don't get the job)

- "Assignment Acknowledgement" (for when you do get the job)

- "Thank You for the Assignment" (for your scheduler after you have completed the job)

- Report Submission Message (for your mystery shopping contact)

- Touching Base (when you want to remind schedulers or mystery shopping companies you work with of your availability)

These are small touches, but they go a long way in making you memorable to schedulers and portraying yourself as a professional mystery shopper who can be counted upon to do the job in a quality manner. See the Resources section for some sample letters that you can adapt to your own style.

You can further demonstrate your professionalism by doing assignments correctly, handing in well-written reports, and, above all, getting the assignment done and handed in on time. If you are having trouble completing your assignment after doing everything possible to attempt the shop as instructed, do not hesitate to ask the mystery shopping company for additional assistance and guidance. If you are not going to meet the deadline for an assignment, let the company and your scheduler know as soon as possible, to see if an extension is possible, or in case they need to make arrangements to give the job to another shopper who can complete the job in time. The same holds true if you are not going to be able to do a shop at all—you get sick, your car dies, you are called out of town for work, etc. Give both your scheduler and the mystery shopping company as much notice as possible to re-assign the shop.

While it is assumed that if you accept an assignment, you will complete it, life happens and everyone understands (as long as you rarely cancel out on a shop, because then you could end up canceling yourself out of future assignments for good). Giving advance notice immediately will be respected and not knock you out of consideration for the future. That said, always try to do your shops well-ahead of the deadline, so the chances that life will interfere will be a lot lower.

I once was supposed to do an oil change shop with my husband's Mitsubishi® and wouldn't you know it, the morning I was supposed to go for the shop, the car would not start. The car eventually had to be towed to the repair shop and needed a new starter. I immediately contacted my scheduler and let her know what had happened. Not only did she thank me for letting her know so quickly, she was able to work with me to extend the deadline for the shop so I was still able to do the assignment.

Here's a word about kids and being a professional. If you are a stay-at-home Mom or Dad, you might be wondering if it's okay to bring your kids along on shops. My advice would be to bring them along if you need to if the kids really are well-behaved. This is a "work-at-home "career" and one of the benefits is the flexibility it can offer you in caring for, and spending time with your kids.

Keep in mind though, part of portraying yourself as a professional mystery shopper is to be focused on your assignment. Since you are being paid to make detailed observations, your ability to do your very best may be compromised if little Joey is running amuck and you are distracted. Some companies also may not permit your children coming along on a particular assignment. Of course in some cases, having a child (or access to one) is helpful or even necessary in order to be able to do an assignment—a toy store shop, a day care center, the babysitting facility at a gym, etc. So overall, use your judgment and be sure to note if an assignment does not permit a child to be taken along. If you are not sure, always ask!

2. Group Assignments Together

This idea is very important for time management so that you can get the most shops in within the time you have to devote to the work each week. Plus, it is key if you do retail shops which often take place in a local mall or major strip center. It is a waste of your time and gas to make a trip for one shop and then have to go back to the same location for another one, and perhaps another one. While scheduling may not always permit, do your best to not do a solo shop in such a location.

Combining assignments may also make a lower paying shop more attractive if it is quick and you can do it with one or two other ones on the same trip. If you can do three $7 to $12 shops in one trip, your hourly rate has now increased substantially. Yet if you did each of them separately with driving time and gas, it would not be worth your time. This holds true even for higher-paying shops. Do your best to do shops that are in the same area together. Also, use the directions web site on Yahoo under the "maps" link to map out the best directions so you can easily go from one location to another as quickly as possible.

3. Try to Get Regular Gigs

While they are rare, sometimes a particular type of shop—especially in retail—will lend itself to using the same shopper for several months. Having steady shops that you know you can count on certainly helps keep your earnings up. Plus, you may be able to take on other assignments in the same area, knowing that you are going there anyway (the "grouping assignments together" strategy) to maximize your earnings.

I once did a weekly and a bi-weekly shop for the same company for two different locations of the same retail store. Each of the two was at a major mall, so not only could I count on their $100 per month, there were always shops from other companies that I could take on at these malls, so my earnings grew steadily. This would also work well for locations in your immediate neighborhood where you do your personal shopping and running of errands every day, or one you go to all the time for other reasons like a doctor's appointment or to work out. This is where taking on a lower-paying, but easy and steady "gig" will make sense.

4. Come to the Rescue of a Scheduler or Mystery Shopping Company

The more flexible your schedule, the more money you'll make. If a mystery shopping company or scheduler knows that you are a good, professional mystery shopper that they can turn to when a rush assignment or cancellation comes in, you will get these assignments offered directly to you without having to compete with other shoppers to get them.

When you get that call or e-mail, jump in immediately if you can possibly re-arrange your schedule that day—especially if it is for a company you have not worked for before. Your grateful mystery shopping company or scheduler will remember how you came to their rescue, and you'll have an "in" with them. In fact while you are in contact, they may just offer you another shop they just received and they haven't even posted anywhere yet!

5. Wait for the Cancellations, Holiday Times or Peak Periods to Increase Your Pay for the Same Assignment

Once you start reading the job lead boards and your e-mail from schedulers regularly, you'll see these familiar words in the subject lines of postings and messages: "HELP!!! Lunch Shop in Anywhere, CA Due Today!" or "Shop With Bonus, Anywhere CA!", "URGENT! Anywhere, CA Shopper Needed Today!" etc. When scanning which e-mails or postings to read out of your growing list, check these out first!

Again, this is another example where being flexible in your schedule will definitely increase your earnings. It's good old supply and demand! When a job has to be completed for a client and there is trouble finding someone to complete it, the money offered to do the job goes up. This happens because a shopper had to cancel an assignment they had previously accepted; an assignment's location is not popular; or a rush job came in from a client. So the same apartment shop you saw going for $25 is now offering a $5 bonus or more. Or maybe that car dealership shop is now worth $40. I have also seen lunch or dinner shops that were reimbursement-only deals, suddenly have a $5 or $10 bonus thrown in. By the way, the food and apartment shops, by far, seem to have the most "cries for help".

Sometimes, just because shops are scheduled during a holiday period, there will be other bonuses offered so the scheduler knows the job will get done as their usually reliable shoppers turn to other things. One Christmas, a scheduler, because she was going on vacation, offered to pay an innovative extra bonus out of her own pocket for service shops that were normally going for $20. The deal was that you would get an extra dollar added to your pay for each day you got the shop report in ahead of the due date. A bonus of up to $7 was available since the deadline was in a week. You better believe that I and the other shoppers who snatched up that assignment got our reports in 6 to 7 days early so we got paid $26 or $27 for that shop rather than $20!

While these "cries for help" can happen anytime, be especially alert at month's end, and during holidays, when the most cancellations and desperate schedulers seem to exist. It's a win-win situation. You help them out, and in return, get paid more than usual for the same assignment. In fact, I have found for certain schedulers that they almost always seem to have a crisis that I can rescue them from, so I stopped putting in for their assignments when they were first posted earlier in the month and waited for the "HELP" e-mail so that I could get better pay for the same assignment. This is easy to do once you already have done a good amount of work for the month so you can be choosier about your jobs as the month progresses. Learn the "crisis" patterns in your market and profit from them.

6. Focus on Service Assignments

As I mentioned earlier, service shops and dinner restaurant shops (in reimbursement) tend to pay the most as they are the most complex and usually require a page or two of narrative. These are your apartment, homebuilder, office space, gym, car dealer, oil change, financial service shops (and anything else that falls in this category) paying at least $20 to $25 and up.

On another note, service and restaurant shops are also preferable because in doing retail shops you may be tempted to spend the money you're earning, and then some at the local mall or shopping center. You're less likely to spend by doing an apartment shop or bank shop. Be careful at those car dealer shops though—you don't want to let them talk you into a new car (unless you really need one)!

7. Get in as Many Schedulers' Databases as Possible

As you have already seen, I am a big believer in getting known by the schedulers who hold the key to many jobs from many different companies, rather than an individual company that only deals with their own assignments. Although there are also some great schedulers out there worth knowing that just deal in their own companies' jobs. I cannot stress enough how important it is to regularly apply to job leads from schedulers (independent and company-specific) to get in their databases for future assignments. Many schedulers work together and will share your information with their colleagues within their own company, or friends of theirs who are schedulers. Palm and Kern Scheduling alone can keep you busy working. Just one contact can result in a lot of exposure, so think what many contacts will do for you!

In addition, it can't hurt to contact a scheduler for future consideration even if they are not posting a job in your particular area. For example, you see a posting for California, but it's in another part of the state. The chances are the scheduler will handle assignments for other cities in California, or at least within a certain region, but just doesn't have a specific job right now. By making contact in advance, you'll be in their database or possibly referred to a colleague or friend of theirs. Keep in mind though that this should not be abused. I wouldn't contact a scheduler with a Florida job lead posting only and tell her to keep you in mind for California. You can tweak the Job Lead Response Letter in the Resource Section for this purpose.

8. <u>Do Shops When You Travel</u>

Between the job lead boards and the web sites of companies you work with, you will be able to monitor job leads for all over the United States and Canada (and perhaps even abroad). Don't forget that you can also mystery shop when you are in another location away from home either for other work you do, when visiting family, or when traveling on vacation.

Now you probably aren't going to want to do an apartment shop when your trip purpose is to lie on the beach in Hawaii. But maybe there are a couple of lunch or dinner shops you can do so you can help stretch your travel budget and possibly eat at a better place than for which you might have budgeted.

Before you travel, be sure to check out all your usual lead sources to see if there is anything doing in the city you'll be in that appeals to you. Another idea is to drop a quick e-mail to the schedulers you normally work with telling them your travel plans, and asking if they either have, or can keep you in mind, for any assignments in that area. Ask them to please pass that information along to any scheduler colleagues or friends that might handle shops for your travel destination as well.

Tip: There is a special group in Delphi Forums called Reliable Traveling Shoppers located at http://forums.delphiforums.com/travelingms/start. Here you can find shops from companies open to working with shoppers who are traveling to their area, as well as list your future availability in a city to which you are traveling.

9. Be Open to Non-Shopper Jobs

As you do your mystery shopper work, you will also notice that other opportunities for similar flexible schedule, independent contractor work, may come your way. From time-to-time, I see requests for merchandisers, inventory auditors or demonstrators show up on the mystery shopping lead boards and some individual companies also handle this kind of work for their clients.

A <u>merchandiser</u> is someone who goes to retail stores and may be responsible for changing brochures in display racks, setting up promotional displays, delivering some materials, and liaisoning with the store manager. By the way, combining merchandising and mystery shopping creates a dual, home-based career that can't be beat! If you are interested in finding out more information, check out the new merchandising section on my web site at <u>http://www.mysteryshoppercoach.com/merchandising.htm l</u> and my book *The Quick And Easy Guide To Making Money As A Merchandiser* available 24/7 at <u>http://www.mysteryshoppercoach.com/books.html</u>.

An <u>inventory auditor</u> may be asked to do counts of merchandise or possibly re-sticker the pricing on products. Finally, a <u>demonstrator</u> is the person you see in a grocery store, or other retail location who hands out samples and coupons (note this usually involves weekend and night work).

Once you are well known and do excellent work for some of your schedulers and mystery shopping companies, you may be offered the opportunity to provide clerical assistance to a company or a scheduler. Plus, if you write well, you may be given editing assignments to tidy up the written reports of other shoppers who are not as well skilled in written communication as you are. I have received many compliments on my narratives for mystery shops and have picked up such assignments from a couple of companies myself. They are great for reliable income you can count on each month.

You also may be able to eventually become a scheduler yourself once you have proven yourself as a mystery shopper. I have a whole chapter on what it takes to get into scheduling and the pros and cons of this type of work called *Scheduling: The Brass Ring* in my second book *How-To Finally Make Money As A Mystery Shopper.* If you haven't already received that book as part of my Mystery Shopping Two-Volume Set, you can get that book 24/7 at http://www.mysteryshoppercoach.com/books.html.

Any of these "non-shopper" assignments may be something you want to pursue to round out your mystery shopping work and add to your earnings. I always say keep an open mind, make connections, be a professional and you never know what opportunities may present themselves!

10. Stay in Touch With Schedulers or Companies Who You Haven't Worked With in Awhile

Once you get established where you are included in many schedulers' databases; have a few regular mystery shopping companies that you work with; and monitor select job lead sources on a daily basis; you probably will have all the assignments you desire (and them some). But if you are looking for work, it never hurts to drop a quick, polite e-mail reminding a scheduler of:

- work you have done together in the past;

- the cities your shop in;

- the kinds of shops you do; and

- that since you enjoyed working with them in the past, you would be happy to have the opportunity to do so again soon.

This message is basically a version of the Shopper Job Lead Response message. Please see the Resource Section for a sample. I have used this when I have been away on vacation, so I can let everyone know I am back and available. By doing so, I have picked up some assignments to get me up and running again quickly.

Chapter Fourteen: Notes/Questions

Chapter Fifteen: Now That You Know How To Get Started, Get Going!

To put it all together, here's a summary of seven things you need to do to get your mystery shopping career launched:

1. Set Up Your "Home Office" (even if it's the kitchen table)

Decide how you'll handle internet access, faxing and doing your reports. Get your e-mail account established (and create a new e-mail address that is more professional if necessary). Create your professional voicemail message and teach others in your household how to take a proper message for you. Get hold of any software you may need—even freebies like Acrobat Reader® (www.adobe.com) and WinZip® (www.winzip.com).

2. Decide on Your Coverage Area

Know in advance the cities and towns where you are willing to shop, and create a list that you put on your computer in your response message.

3. Review the Resource Section

Create your own sample e-mail messages or responses to job application questions for each type you'll need:

- Sample Response To Job Lead Posting

- "Keep Me in Mind" Response (for when you don't get the job)

- "Assignment Acknowledgement" (for when you do get the job)

- "Thank You for the Assignment" (for your scheduler after you have completed the job)

- Report Submission Message (for your mystery shopping company contact)

- Touching Base (when you want to remind schedulers or mystery shopping companies you work with of your availability)

- Sample Answers to the Five Commonly Asked Questions on Web site

- Applications

4. <u>Start Visiting the Suggested Job Lead Sources</u>

I suggest visiting your top two or three resources frequently at first until you are in many schedulers' databases. Others you can check more to keep tabs on. The more job leads you apply for at first, the more jobs you'll land and the more contacts you'll make *so the jobs will eventually find you!* Don't forget that you need to respond to job lead postings right away to have the best chance of landing the assignment. Also, don't be too picky on pay or type of shop, and possibly be willing to drive a little further at first to get those initial assignment "credits" under your belt.

Later on, as an experienced shopper you can be more selective (and this isn't years away—if you've done at least 10 jobs well, especially ones with lengthy narratives, you're experienced). Once you are established, check your e-mail every two or three hours ideally—even in the evening—as those e-mails now represent chances to earn money or eat at your favorite restaurant for free! You should land your first assignment within your first few days of a consistent effort where you immediately respond to leads.

5. Apply to Some Mystery Shopping Companies Directly

Remember, there is only one time it pays to apply directly to a mystery shopping company. To learn the secret, go to: http://www.mysteryshoppercoach.com/secretsites.html You don't want to apply to just any old company, and certainly not a couple of hundred, a hundred or even 50 companies. If you work the lead boards/lists and sign up with Kern and Palm Scheduling Services, you will have made much more valuable independent and company scheduler contacts, and have job leads e-mailed to you on a regular basis soon enough.

6. Set Up Records

Get organized and keep track of scheduler contacts made; companies you have signed up with (including passwords or shopper ID information); your shop assignments; and payments due. Again, please e-mail me at Melanie@mysteryshoppercoach.com for my free, cool Excel spreadsheets that will help you get organized and save you time.

7. Sign up for my free e-zine "*Perfect Work-At-Home Job Update*"

E-mail me at mscoach@aweber.com. In my e-zine I answer select questions from my readers, and share some of my latest tips and news from the trenches—*the inside scoop that you've been looking for, but no one tells you*. Also be sure to regularly check out my web site Mystery Shopper Coach's Corner at http://www.mysteryshoppercoach.com for back issues of my e-zine, tips, resources, special offers and more!

Chapter Fifteen: Notes/Questions

Chapter Sixteen: Final Thoughts

So there you have it—everything you need to become a successful mystery shopper. If you make the effort and prove yourself, before you know it, you'll be just like I was—with more jobs and related income opportunities coming your way than you can handle. Just don't forget that the whole purpose of doing this kind of flexible work is to use it to give yourself the life you desire. Use this flexibility to take time for yourself, your friends and loved ones, and to do the things you always say you would do "if you had more time".

Good luck with your new work-at-home career as a mystery shopper! If you would like to share with me your success stories about becoming a mystery shopper, how you, as an experienced shopper have improved your income using the ideas in this book, or how the flexibility of mystery shopping has improved your life, I'd love to hear from you! E-mail me at Melanie@mysteryshoppercoach.com.

And when you're ready to take the next step in your career, be sure to get your copy of my book *How-To Finally Make Money As A Mystery Shopper* which includes detailed chapters on scheduling, finding specialized types of shops, doing video mystery shopping and power negotiating for higher shop fees. If you enjoyed this book you'll love *How-To Finally Make Money As A Mystery Shopper!* And to really maximize your income, create a dual, flexible, home-based career by adding merchandising work to your mystery shopping. It's easy to do with my book *The Quick And Easy Guide To*

Making Money As A Merchandiser. More information about merchandising and FAQs can be found at my web site Mystery Shopper Coach's Corner at http://www.mysteryshoppercoach.com/merchandising.html. Please see the Resource Section for ordering information.

—*Melanie R. Jordan*

P.S. As a special thank you for purchasing this book, I want to be sure you are kept up-to-date on any changes that many occur to some of the resources listed. Please check this special URL for any updates from time-to-time provided FREE to you!
http://www.mysteryshoppercoach.com/updates.html

P.P.S. I am constantly writing and publishing new books and special reports on a variety of topics. Please check my publishing company's web site at http://www.sunloverpublishing.com for other publications you might enjoy.

Resource Section

I. Sample E-Mail Correspondence

1. Sample Response To Job Lead Posting

Re: Anywhere, CA Apartment Shop

Jane—

I saw your message on the Mystery Shoppers Resource web site and am available to help you with the Anywhere, CA apartment shop due June 7th. If this shop is no longer available, I would greatly appreciate your adding me to your database for future assignments.

Currently, I am regularly working with eight companies on a regular basis—Joey's Mystery Shopping, ABC Shopping, XYZ Shoppers, 123 Service, Joey's Spies, Service/Service, The Jane Doe Group and Made-Up Mystery Shopping (apartment, restaurant, retail, automotive, fitness center and other service-type shops). I am self-employed as a writer and editor with flexible hours weekdays.

With 20+ years experience in marketing and an extensive background in market research, customer service and sales training, I am a valuable asset to any research firm. I have also worked in the financial services industry and in retailing. I am observant, detail-oriented, dependable, have excellent communication skills and am PC literate.

I especially focus on shops in these cities:

Anywhere, Anyplace Forest, Anytime, Nowhere Ranch, Sometime, Shopper Viejo, Mystery Beach, Service Mesa, Somewhere and Secret Point

Thank you for your time and consideration. I look forward to being of service!

Melanie Jordan
Melanie@mysteryshoppercoach.com

2. "Keep Me In Mind" Response (For When You Don't Get The Job)

Re: Your Last Message

Jane—

Thank you for getting back to me about the Anywhere, CA apartment shop. I am sorry to hear that the assignment was already filled. However, please be sure to let me know if you have a cancellation—with my flexible schedule I can usually jump right in on an assignment that another shopper was unable to deliver.

I would also greatly appreciate you adding me to your database of shoppers and keeping me in mind for future assignments. Again, I am a reliable and experienced shopper focusing on assignments in Anywhere, Anyplace Forest, Anytime, Nowhere Ranch, Sometime, Shopper Viejo, Mystery Beach, Service Mesa, Somewhere and Secret Point, CA.

Thank you for your time and consideration. I look forward to working with you soon.

Melanie Jordan
Melanie@mysteryshoppercoach.com

Note: if you have not yet had even a single shop (once you've had at least one you can truthfully say you have experience), just say I focus on assignments in…and leave out the phrase about being an experienced shopper.

3. "Assignment Acknowledgement" (For When You Do Get The Job)

Re: Anywhere, CA Apartment Shop Confirmation

Jane—

Thank you for the apartment shop assignment in Anywhere, CA due June 7th at a pay rate of $25. You can count on me to meet your deadline, and I appreciate the opportunity to work with you and Joey's Mystery Shopping.

Melanie Jordan
Melanie@mysteryshoppercoach.com

Note: if this is a scheduler or company you work with fairly regularly, you can make your phrasing a little more personal like "it's always a pleasure to work with you and Joey's Mystery Shopping". Or "nice to be working with you and Joey's Mystery Shopping again".

4. "Thank You For The Assignment" After You Have Completed The Job (To Your Scheduler)

Re: Anywhere, CA Apartment Shop Completed

Jane—

I just wanted to let you know this shop was completed today and I just sent the report to Mary Jones at Joey's Mystery Shopping.

Thank you for the opportunity, and I look forward to working with you again soon. Please keep me in your database for future assignments.

Melanie Jordan
Melanie@mysteryshoppercoach.com

5. Report Submission Message (To The Actual Mystery Shopping Company Contact)

Re: Anywhere, CA—Jones Shop Completed

Mary—

Attached are two documents—one contains the Excel forms Jane Doe provided me with for this shop; the other is a separate word document with the shop narrative. Please let me know if you have any questions or difficulty with the attachments.

I greatly appreciated the opportunity to be of service for

this assignment and I look forward to working with you again soon.

Melanie Jordan
Melanie@mysteryshoppercoach.com

Note: if this is a company you work with fairly regularly, you can make your phrasing a little more personal like "it's always a pleasure to work with you". Or "nice to be working with you again".

6. Touching Base (Looking For Work)

Re: Touching Base (or Checking In)

Hi Jane—

I recently did some apartment shops for you in Anywhere, Somewhere and Secret Point, CA. Since I have some extra time in my schedule over the next few days and enjoyed working with you, I was wondering if there were any assignments that I could help you with?

Again, I am a reliable and experienced shopper focusing on assignments in Anywhere, Anyplace Forest, Anytime, Nowhere Ranch, Sometime, Shopper Viejo, Mystery Beach, Service Mesa, Somewhere and Secret Point, CA.

Thank you for your time and consideration. I look forward to working with you again soon.

Melanie Jordan
Melanie@mysteryshoppercoach.com

II. Mystery Shopping Company Application Question & Answer Samples

1. Why Do You Mystery Shop/Want To Be A Mystery Shopper?

I am an experienced mystery shopper and I do it for two primary reasons:

1. I have a strong desire to see that companies provide the best possible customer service.

2. I like having the opportunity to supplement my income with interesting, enjoyable work with flexible hours.

2. Why Do Companies Use Mystery Shoppers?

Mystery shoppers are the objective eyes and ears of the store owners or management and can provide valuable feedback that can be used in many ways including: improving customer service, identifying sales training needs and tying in to employee performance evaluations.

3. What Would You Do If Someone Asked If You Were A Shopper?

I would look confused and say "what's that, I have no idea of what you mean"? If pressed after they explained what a shopper was, I would of course deny it. Then I would ask a question that was appropriate for the situation to focus attention back on the customer experience and change the subject.

4. Describe Your Worst (A Poor) Customer Service Experience

<u>An Example of a Poor Customer Service Experience</u>

My worst shopping experience was recently at my local Market. It was a Tuesday afternoon about 4:00. There were only 3 check-outs open and I was in a hurry. I got on one line and the person checking out started fighting with the cashier about the price of an item and was yelling loud enough for everyone to hear. I got off that line in a hurry!

I went to the next one, and just as I re-loaded my items on the conveyor belt, the cashier switched off her light waiting for a manager to appear—she didn't know how to ring up a gift certificate. In disgust, I went to the last and only open line. Here were two cashiers—one was training the other and the person ringing was scanning the items slower than you would think was humanly possible. Then disaster struck, a can of Pringles was ringing up at a different price than the sales price! The cashier tried voiding, re-keying several times and it wasn't working. The customer wanted to cancel the purchase and the cashier couldn't get it to void even with the help of her "trainer" so now we were all stuck. After trying to check out for 35 minutes on 3 lines, I gave up and left.

5. Describe Your Best (A Positive) Customer Service Experience

<u>An Example of A Positive Customer Service Experience</u>

I believe good customer service is exemplified by my recent experience with Credit Card Claims on my CD player. This is a unit of The Credit Card Company that doubles the manufacturer's warranty on purchases made with their credit card. Everyone I dealt with from the initial representative who answered the phone, through the actual claims reviewer, were polite, informative and not only met my expectations, but exceeded them. I expected a hassle, but instead they took the initiative to keep me informed of my claim's progress; got back to me when they said they would; and even offered a tip that a DVD player would now be permissible to get as a replacement under my claim since this new technology also played CDs.

III. Sample On-Site Narrative For Shopper Report

**Anywhere, CA Apartment Shop
On-Site Presentation
Jane Doe
Shopper: Melanie Jordan**

When I walked in, I was immediately greeted by a female employee who cheerfully asked if she could help me (yes, appointment with Jane). She pointed out Jane who was just finishing up with someone. The employee introduced herself as Mary—she invited me to sit at an adjoining desk and offered me refreshments. Shortly afterwards, Jane walked over, smiled, extended her hand, introduced herself and welcomed me by name.

Jane did a good job of showing the property amenities. For example, when pointing out the resort-style pool, she mentioned how it was heated all year but they turned the temperature down if it got hot in the summer. I also saw the main spa, fitness center (where she greeted another resident working out) and the laundry room ("good for washing your blankets"). We made small talk as we walked over to the model that reinforced the positives of the property like the quiet.

At the model, Jane walked me through and pointed out the features and benefits—loads of closet space, unusual angled patio that was private, white washed cabinets, cozy living room, mirrored closets in bedrooms, room sizes (showed how the smaller one was a very nice size for my home office) and how modern everything was. She asked me how I liked it and I told her I thought it would work very nicely depending on where the actual unit was. I also asked Jane if there were any specials that she could offer because while the unit was nice, it was at the upper end of my price range. She addressed this by saying that the unit actually was on special ($1,380 vs. $1,475) and I would get $300 off move-in with a 6-month lease and $600 off with a 9-month lease.

Jane then asked me to walk with her to see the vacant apartment that was ready now on the second floor so I could see one that was not a model (we did). She next invited me to see the actual unit location of #133 that was occupied, but we walked around the back and up the stairs. My concern about this was the terrace was dark so the exposure was not sunny (she addressed this by telling me the sun would make it too hot in the summer anyway). I told Jane that everything else was right so maybe I could compromise on the terrace.

Back at the office, Jane asked me to fill out an application and leave a $100 deposit to take the unit off the market. I explained I still had two more appointments that day that I wanted to keep. Jane stressed that I wasn't going to find another 2 bedroom like this for $1,380 and the deposit was refundable within 72 hours so I could look and then change my mind. I declined but said I would be deciding in the next day or so. Jane then said to let her know as soon as possible because she "couldn't say that unit would still be there". I assured her I would, and she stood, smiled, extended her hand and thanked me for coming in.

Overall, I thought Jane did a good job with the tour of the property and the apartment. Jane listened carefully to my needs, did her best to counter my objections and tried to close me multiple times. Had I really been looking for an apartment, I would have leased from her.

IV. Ordering Additional Copies of The Perfect Work-At-Home Job: Mystery Shopping

Melanie's classic 162-page book *The Perfect Work-At-Home Job: Mystery Shopping* is a great resource for the newbie or beginning shopper, as well as those who might never have otherwise thought about the possibility of mystery shopping as a work-at-home career. It's a great gift idea! It may be purchased 24/7 as follows:

For a pdf file viewable by PC or Mac using Adobe Acrobat's reader (available as a free download from www.adobe.com if you don't have it), go to:

http://www.booklocker.com/books/923.html

Please cut and paste the URL into your browser and then hit enter.

Please note that all of these e-book files go through a complete virus scan before they are made available for download on Booklocker.com (my book sales site host). You can count on the file you download to be clean and safe.

To make an e-book purchase using PayPal™ funds, a check or money order, please e-mail me at Melanie@mysteryshoppercoach.com for instructions on making your purchase directly through me.

Here's what others are saying about this book:

"I bought both of your mystery shopping books 3 weeks ago and they've helped me get off to a great start. I booked 11 shops for $290 in shop fees and $162 in restaurant reimbursements for a total of $452!"--C. Wilson, Los Angeles, CA

"The day I bought your book changed my life! I have followed your advice, almost to the letter, and it has paid off in spades. In the last three weeks I have done over 35 mystery shops and I am currently scheduled to perform approximately fifteen more over the next week. Many of the shops I have completed included bonuses for upcoming deadlines or remote areas."-- Patrick B., Richmond, VA

"Thanks again for providing a great book for those who want to become mystery shoppers. Friday night I started following your tips and visiting the suggested websites. I was offered my first mystery shopping job on Monday morning! Since then, I have accepted two more and actually completed my first job!"--M.S., Louisville, KY

"I think the resources you provide to mystery shoppers are incredibly valuable. I put your advice into practice and accepted my first apartment shop. I had a blast and have completed 8 more apartment shops and a fitness shop. I spent under $30 for both books and the apartment shops more than made up for it at $20-$30 apiece!"--H. Lewis, Vancouver, WA

"I just purchased both of your mystery shopping books and am pleased to say that I already got a transportation shop and two retail shops. Thank you for all of the advice on how to get started the right way. You stress the importance of being both professional and organized, and I cannot agree with you more.--Ann-Marie M., Atlanta, GA

V. About How-To Finally Make Money As A Mystery Shopper

Melanie's follow-up book is *How-To Finally Make Money As A Mystery Shopper*. This 140-page resource is designed to help the experienced shopper who just isn't making the money they desire get to that next level of mystery shopper earnings.

It takes the best of the material from *The Perfect Work-At-Home Job: Mystery Shopping* and adds chapters, tips and resources you won't want to miss! Plus, the content-packed chapters called *Power Negotiating For Higher Mystery Shopper Fees* and a section on *Getting What's Coming To You*, along with ones on scheduling, video mystery shopping and finding specialized shops that alone are worth the price of the book.

Please note that there is some overlap of material between the two books, but there is lots of unique content in each. Check out the table of contents on-line at the URLs listed below to see if this book is for you. You can also order one for your experienced shopper friends and family—it's a great gift idea! It may be purchased 24/7 as follows.

For a pdf file viewable by PC or Mac using Adobe Acrobat's reader (available as a free download from www.adobe.com if you don't have it), go to:

http://www.booklocker.com/books/924.html

Please cut and paste the URL into your browser and then hit enter.

Please note that all of these e-book files go through a complete virus scan before they are made available for download on Booklocker.com (my book sales site host). You can count on the file you download to be clean and safe!

To make an e-book purchase using PayPal™ funds, a check or money order, please e-mail me at Melanie@mysteryshoppercoach.com for instructions on making your purchase directly through me.

What others are saying about this book:

"I loved your book! Thanks for all the great leads and hints. I have used all your ideas and techniques and so far have received 11 new assignments in the last 18 days!"--Lara O., Arlington Heights, IL

"I used one of your tips about getting more money for shops at the end of the month and I received $35 and $32 for two shops that normally pay $25 apiece! This is the best part-time job I have ever had."--Vicky M., Seattle, WA

"You have put together a well-written, wonderful resource that is a pleasure to read and is offering me so much information that I just didn't have before. I applaud you for a great book!"--J. Knight, Boston, MA

VI. About The Quick And Easy Guide To Making Money As A Merchandiser

Order additional copies of *The Quick And Easy Guide To Making Money As A Merchandiser* for your friends, family and even your fellow mystery shoppers—it's a great gift idea! It may be purchased 24/7 as follows:

For a pdf file viewable by PC or Mac using Adobe Acrobat's reader (available as a free download from www.adobe.com if you don't have it), go to:

http://www.booklocker.com/books/948.html

Please cut and paste the URL into your browser and then hit enter.

Please note that all of these e-book files go through a complete virus scan before they are made available for download on Booklocker.com (my book sales site host). You can count on the file you download to be clean and safe.

Or for a print copy of this book, it's also available from Booklocker.com at:

http://www.booklocker.com/books/948.html

To purchase this e-book using PayPal™ funds, a check or money order, please e-mail me at Melanie@mysteryshoppercoach.com for instructions on making your purchase directly through me.

Here's what others are saying about this book:

"I purchased your book "The Quick And Easy Guide To Making Money As A Merchandiser" a few days ago and just today I received my first assignment. And it's a year-round situation doing resets/revisions in a local store. I truly appreciate your book!"--Chell S., Tyler, TX

"I ordered your book on Saturday, read the whole thing and started using the information the next day. On Wednesday I got my first assignment for a major discount retailer! On Friday I got another job to do at two other stores near my home. I can't believe how quickly I got leads in my area. Thank you for the great book and great new career!"--Natalie B., Weston, WI

"Your book is packed with great ideas and suggestions--I couldn't put it down! I found the merchandising field was a pretty closely guarded secret, for which it was very hard to get any information. That is why I like and appreciate your book so much!"--Helen P., Jacksonville, FL

VII. About Secret Mystery Shopping Sites Revealed!

Available by special order only at Melanie's web site Mystery Shopper Coach's Corner at http://www.mysteryshoppercoach.com/secretsites.html.

How would you like to actually know that you have a mystery shopping assignment when you see one announced, rather than wait to have it assigned to you? How about the ability to work more efficiently by grouping assignments together? Or even a way to hear about mystery shopping assignments in even the smallest cities and towns?

There's a new way to get some of your mystery shopping assignments, and when you combine it with the sure-fire techniques I discuss in *The Perfect Work-At-Home Job: Mystery Shopping* and *How-To Finally Make Money As A Mystery Shopper*, you'll be able to take control of your mystery shopper income and career like never before! Get your copy of *Secret Mystery Shopping Sites Revealed!* today at http://www.mysteryshoppercoach.com/secretsites.html.

What others are saying about this book:
"Great shopping tips! I devoured your book "Secret Mystery Shopping Sites Revealed!" I guess I was off to a good start, but I was able to get some very helpful info, new leads and tips."—D. Krohn, Bristol, RI

"Thank you for your precious and valuable insights!"--
Trevis B., Brooklyn, NY

VIII. Ever Thought About Starting Your Own Mystery Shopping Business But Didn't Know Where To Start?

A popular question I am often asked by both experienced and newbie mystery shoppers alike is "what does it take to start my own mystery shopping business"?

Well, for the answer, I recently had the pleasure of interviewing author and veteran mystery shopping business owner, Shari Joseph who graciously shared her experiences in running her own mystery shopping business, and how you can start one too! Read the interview here:

http://www.mysteryshoppercoach.com/mysteryshoppingbusiness2.html

You can order Shari's book 24/7 using this URL:

http://www.mystery-shopper-business.com/affiliations/mj.html

Plus, if you want to really jump-start your own mystery shopping business, Shari now has a complete kit that contains "plug in your information" contracts, ready made Microsoft® Word questionnaire templates, tracking logs, letterhead, business cards and lots more! Check it out at this URL:

http://www.mystery-shopper-business.com/affiliations/mjKit.html

About Melanie R. Jordan

Melanie left Corporate America to practice what she preaches: achieving a more satisfying and flexible existence with "work that fits her life, not the other way around". Today, based on her business world life lessons, everything she does is only done on her terms.

As a firm believer that the secret to successful self-employment is to have several streams of flexible income, Melanie uses all her talents and experience across a diverse field of self-employed endeavors.

Melanie has 20+ years experience in marketing from her work with some of the country's largest banks, as well as over eight years of experience in direct sales and customer service in the fields of real estate and loans. Her exposure to these two fields led to her establishment of two successful mentoring programs: one for new real estate agents for a small, independent California real estate brokerage, and the other for a national, entrepreneurial marketing and training company in the financial services field.

Melanie is also much in demand as an independent, home-based marketing and infopreneur consultant, sales trainer and coach for small businesses.

However, her biggest passion is writing about, and coaching others on, a variety of topics that she is passionate about related to work-at-home lifestyles, health and fitness, infopreneuring and marketing. She is also the author *of Have Your Cheeseburger And Keep*

Your Health Too! Check out Melanie's other web site "Healthy Eating Coach's Corner" at www.healthyeatingcoach.com for more information about her approach to healthy living. All of her works are published with the in-depth, "tell it like it really is" style, that has attracted fans across North America and in many other countries throughout the world.

She also publishes a free e-zine for mystery shoppers and merchandisers called *The Perfect Work-At-Home Job Update* where she answers select questions from her readers and shares some of her latest tips and news from the trenches (subscribe by sending an e-mail to mscoach@aweber.com).

Melanie welcomes your comments, questions and suggestions and can be reached at Melanie@mysteryshoppercoach.com.

And since she is constantly writing and publishing new books and special reports on a variety of topics, please check her publishing company's web site at http://www.sunloverpublishing.com for other publications you might enjoy.

How-To Finally Make Money
As A Mystery Shopper

By
Melanie R. Jordan

Fourth Edition, Revised 11/07

How-To Finally Make Money As A Mystery Shopper
By Melanie R. Jordan

Fourth Edition, Revised 11/07

Published By
SunLover Publishing

e-mail: Melanie@mysteryshoppercoach.com

Perfect Work-At-Home Job Update free monthly e-zine
subscription e-mail: mscoach@aweber.com

Mystery Shopper Coach's Corner Web Site:
http://www.mysteryshoppercoach.com

SunLover Publishing publishes books on a number of "how-to"
topics related to work-at-home lifestyles, infopreneuring,
marketing and health and fitness. Check out our web site at
http://www.SunLoverPublishing.com for other publications that
may be of interest to you.

Melanie R. Jordan may be contacted by e-mail or mail using
the information provided above regarding this book (including
permission to reproduce selections).

Disclaimer

This book offers information on the subject matter indicated by the title. It is not intended to substitute for legal or other professional advice. Readers should consult with a professional whenever expert advice is needed. As laws and regulations may change from time to time, it is recommended that readers contact the appropriate authority to assure compliance with applicable statutes.

The author and publisher shall assume no responsibility or liability with respect to any loss or damage caused, or alleged to be caused, by the application of the information contained in this book.

If you feel a need to share this book, please do so with a reputable newsletter for review. Please don't copy it to give away. You're getting the benefit of my experience, which will give you a nice work-at-home income forever if you so desire, at a very reasonable price. Please allow me to earn a living so I can continue to create valuable books for you.

This book is dedicated to the world's best husband—my husband, Rich—for his complete support in my quest to become the writer I always knew I could be. As always, "thank you for loving me".

Table of Contents

How This Book Will Help You Finally Make Money As A Mystery Shopper

If you're reading this book, you have some experience in mystery shopping but you just aren't making the money you feel you should. (If you're a newbie or beginner, you first need my other book *The Perfect Work At-Home-Job: Mystery Shopping* if you didn't already get this book as part of my *Mystery Shopping 2-Volume Set*. It's available 24/7 at http://www.mysteryshoppercoach.com/books.html. Based on my work with other shoppers, you probably fall into one of the following groups:

1. <u>You've got "paid to shop, eat for free" syndrome</u>. Too many mystery shoppers focus on this side of mystery shopping. It may be fun, but you pay a high price in terms of earning money to be a mall rat or a fast food junkie. Besides, there are many other shops out there that are fun too and pay a lot better.

2. <u>You're an experienced shopper who has hit a plateau</u>—much like when you work out or try to lose weight. You've had some success, but you have not reached your goals. Assuming your goals are realistic for the amount of time and effort you are willing to put in; you are open to doing other kinds of shops; and there is good market demand in your area (or one that is reasonably close by), you just need some help to break through and reach your maximum earnings potential.

As you'll see in this book, I have a different view of mystery shopping. I don't buy a lot of the methods that others publicize out there that to me are the ways of the past that don't work and are inefficient. That's okay, I've always been someone who was able to "think outside of the box" as they used to say in my Corporate America days (is it any wonder I saw the light and got out of it)?

I feel it is that reliance on the past that causes so many shoppers to contact me to say "I've been doing mystery shopping, but I can't seem to make any money at it". That's why I wrote this book. Don't worry, after reading it and putting the material to use, you will finally make money as a mystery shopper—and far more than the cost of this book—if you make the effort and are any good as a mystery shopper at all.

Some things may be a review to you, but if you're like me, you believe that one good idea that lands you an assignment, or results in a connection for work that you didn't have before, is always worthwhile. Besides, often when you aren't where you should be, you are making basic mistakes that need to be corrected so it helps to backtrack just a little. Other things will be new to you, because they are based on marketing and business etiquette from the business world.

So here's what you'll learn:

- how-to get your home office in order so you can focus on your mystery shopping work;

- how-to set new earnings goals and reach them;

- how-to expand into higher-paying video and audio mystery shopping;

- insights into the world of scheduling and how to get your big break;

- top secret—how to track down the companies that do specialized shops for travel, audio/video shopping and related opportunities like focus groups;

- power negotiating for higher shop fees;

- 9 things that drain your mystery shopper income;

- how-to avoid making mistakes in your reporting and post-shop activities that cost you future jobs and money;

- the key contacts you must make to be a top earning mystery shopper (and have assignments *coming to you*);

- how to stand out from the crowd and keep yourself in high demand;

- the 6 must-have pieces of e-mail correspondence you need to create to get more jobs and make crucial connections;

- 9 ways to maximize your mystery shopper income;

- *and so much more that it's time to stop listing everything and get you into the "meat" of this book.*

You can also subscribe to my free monthly e-zine *Perfect Work-At-Home Job Update* (a former National Center For Professional Mystery Shoppers (NCPMS) Winner Best Newsletter) by sending an e-mail to me at mscoach@aweber.com. In my e-zine I answer select questions from my readers and share some of my latest tips and news from the trenches—*the inside scoop that you've been looking for, but no one tells you.* Also be sure to regularly check out my web site Mystery Shopper Coach's Corner at http://www.mysteryshoppercoach.com for back issues of my e-zine, tips, resources, special offers and more!

Chapter One: Is Your Home Office Hurting Your Mystery Shopping Work?

I believe that kicking your mystery shopping earnings into high gear begins at home—your home office, that is. Your current set-up might need some tweaking to help you work most efficiently and say to the industry "I'm a professional mystery shopper, you can count on me"! I always tell shoppers to be a professional, even if you are working at home. In fact, go overboard to act professional, as home-based workers often are not taken seriously (jealousy from those who trudge into an office I suppose). You do not want to give anyone a reason to have this perception.

1. Your Home "Office Space"

I advise new mystery shoppers that anything can be their home office—even their kitchen table. However, once you are a serious shopper, committed to making the "big bucks" in the field, you need a little space just for yourself. If you haven't done so already, make setting up your home office a priority.

You want to be able to concentrate when writing reports and sending out assignment-winning e-mails. If you do get a business call, you want to have a quiet place to talk without all kinds of background noise that detracts from your conversation and makes you look like an amateur. Use your den, spare bedroom, part of the garage or a dining room that you never use for dining in anyway, to set yourself up in. Keep it simple and keep it separate. You don't have to spend a fortune on a desk and chair set-up—your furnishings can be from Target, Wal-Mart or Staples (note—this is a possible tax deduction, as is the section of your home you use exclusively for your home office—see chapter 2 "A Word About Taxes").

2. Your Filing System

My husband would laugh really hard at this because my filing system is a bit of a mystery to him (pun intended). All things being equal, I will never be organized when clutter will do. But when there is money at stake, I can be the most organized person around!

I like to keep it simple and make a folder for each company that I am working with. Some shoppers also like to set up folders by date or month. The inside of the folder is good for jotting any notes you want to make about the company. A small, inexpensive filing cabinet can be used to store the folders, or just simply put a rubber band around each one and stack them neatly on a bookshelf or storage unit. For items to keep in your company folders, see Chapter 8 *Are You Making Costly Mistakes In Your Reporting And Post-Shop Activities?*

I have also created two Excel® spreadsheets that assist me in staying very organized. One helps you track post-shop information such as:

- shops completed;

- payment due dates;

- when you can do the shop again (if restrictions apply); and

- a running total of how much you are earning during the month.

The other one is helpful for tracking your mystery shopping contacts such as:

- a list of companies and schedulers you have applied to;

- each company's web site address;

- the date you applied;

- password or user name that you created or were assigned from the company for future access;

- whether or not the company posts their job leads on their web site;

- how often leads are updated; and

- does the company e-mail you when a local assignment is available?

As you'll see, I am not a big fan of applying directly with mystery shopping company web sites in many cases. However, even if you get an assignment through other means, you usually then have to be registered on that company's web site to get paid, so you will have company contacts for that purpose.

I'll be happy to e-mail you free copies of both spreadsheets if you contact me at <u>Melanie@mysteryshoppercoach.com</u>. Remember, you must have Microsoft® Excel software to be able to use them.

3. <u>Your Voicemail</u>

Most companies will handle everything by e-mail, but some like to pick up the phone—especially if it's a rush assignment, or perhaps it's the first time they are working with you. You want to be able to get their messages in a reliable way—not missing the call or having to count on anyone else in your household to take down the right message. Voicemail sounds professional and it's usually very cheap or often free with VoIP services. Also, a message will get through even if your line is busy.

Does your message sound professional? Whatever method you use, make a professional recording *like "you've reached the office of _____. Please leave a message with the best time to return your call and I'll get back to you as soon as possible. Thank you for calling."* No background music; no babies wailing; no joint recordings with your kid, boyfriend, girlfriend or spouse; and no cutesy jokes or other voices.

If you have a cell phone (and these days who doesn't), that is very helpful as you can get calls for another assignment (handled tactfully of course), while you are working a job! Again, keep it professional—don't have one of those songs that answer the phone first delaying access to you from someone who is thinking of offering you an assignment!

In answering your phone during standard business hours, answer it like you would an office phone. Don't just say "hello". Answer with your name or "Hello, this is (your name)." Your friends and family will get used to it—after teasing you unmercifully of course. Don't worry about it, you're trying to make money working at home and your home phone has now become a business tool.

4. Your E-mail Account

Sure you may have one or more e-mail accounts, but do you have a separate e-mail address or screen name (if on AOL) just for your mystery shopping work that is directed to you personally? If you follow my lead-generating methods used in this book you will eventually get a lot of e-mails representing an opportunity to earn money and you don't want them buried in with junk messages about "how to lose 20 pounds by tomorrow", an offer for a free psychic reading and the latest joke your best friend sent you. You also don't want a dual name or family name e-mail address (i.e. jackanddiane@xyz.com or smithfamily@xyz.com so you can be taken seriously. Also avoid inappropriate names like loverboy@xyz.com. Act like a professional. You'll then be treated like one and get more assignments offered to you than you can handle!

5. Your Internet Access

Are you using a reliable internet service provider? At this point, I really would suggest a DSL line or cable modem high-speed service. The extra efficiency and reliability is very helpful and it lets you have VoIP phone service which usually saves you a ton on long distance an calling features. So overall, you might actually save money switching to high-speed.

6. Your Office Equipment

I assume you have computer access because most of you are reading this book as an e-publication. How about other equipment?

You should ideally have your own printer. If not, at least reliable printer access. This is, of course, to print out your assignment confirmations, reports for your records and copies of forms that are e-mailed to you to be used for your shops. Electronic documentation is great, but having electronic AND hard copy back-up never hurts.

You do not absolutely have to have your own fax, as long as you have fax access somehow through a local UPS® Store or other source, a fax program in your computer or one of the fax services on the internet like Efax®. Even if you e-mail all your reports, unless you have a scanner (you don't need one but it's convenient at times if you do), when you must send in receipts from a shop or a business card as proof of going to the assignment site, you have to copy and fax them in. Also, there are still some companies who work with faxed reports. They will fax the assignment to you and you will fax it back (no penalty in the amount you are paid), so fax access is needed.

You don't need a copier. Simply buy some copies in advance from a local, nearby place like the UPS® Store, or the reasonably-priced self-service of a Staples and save. Plus, a copier is a hassle to maintain—let it be someone else's headache. Although, if you have a printer or fax machine, it likely lets you do light copying, so you've got the basics handled.

If you have any or all of these items, you're a step ahead of the game and have a more luxurious home office. I do because I was "lucky". I am a former Vice President of Marketing for one of the country's top financial corporations who got caught up in a consolidating industry and a merger of giants. For all my hard work, I received the old "terminated due to merger", a.k.a. layoff, a.k.a. downsized, a.k.a. "thanks for your eight years of service and loyalty, don't let the door hit you in the butt on the way out". But one thing that was fortunate, was that I was telecommuting when this happened back in 1997, so I negotiated to keep the entire home office set-up they got for me as part of my severance, and then as I made money and my old technology bit the dust, I upgraded.

For you, as an experienced shopper who has yet to earn good money, use the equipment guidelines I noted, and add to your set-up as funds permit and your work requires.

7. Your Software

You don't need fancy software, and you probably have some form of word processing software (yes Microsoft® Word is the typical standard). Do you have Microsoft® Excel spreadsheet software? You've likely noticed that many forms used for shops are pre-formatted using this popular software by the mystery shopping companies and their clients.

If you don't have Excel, some companies will fax you forms and still give you the assignment. But if you fax in reports, you might be losing money because you're often paid less for the assignment since the company will have to re-type your report to edit and compile it for their clients. You also might not get an assignment if you don't have the ability to work with Excel documents, so try not to give yourself a disadvantage if you can help it. By the way, you do not have to be a computer whiz or know how to make a spreadsheet, you simply need to know how to enter data and save it—the mystery shopping company or scheduler will send you the formatted document.

There are only two other software programs you should have if you don't already:

- WinZip®

  It is used to open zip files (what else). WinZip may be needed to open up larger or multiple documents that have been compressed for e-mailing to speed up the amount of time they take to download. It is a freebie that you can download from www.winzip.com (choose the free demo version).

- Adobe Acrobat® Reader

If you didn't buy this book as a pdf file, then you need to know about this. Some forms or documents to be read like company-specific training materials, or guidelines for the particular shop, may be in a format that is made with Adobe software that creates what is known as a "pdf" file. You need to be able to access such files that are sent to you or that you are asked to view on a company's web site. This is another freebie available at www.adobe.com. If you try to open a document that is in pdf format, the software senses this and automatically opens it for you—it's as simple as that.

Chapter One: Notes/Questions

Chapter Two: A Word About Taxes

I've included this section because I still get lots of questions about taxes from experienced shoppers—maybe I should become a CPA! Let me start this section off with the disclaimer that I am not a tax professional, and that you should verify the following information with your own tax advisor as regulations are constantly changing, and everyone's tax situation is unique. Now that I have gotten that out of the way, here is a basic idea of what it means to be an independent contractor from a tax point-of-view.

First, you are considered self-employed, which means that you will receive a form 1099 at year-end to let the IRS know what you have earned rather than a W-2. Please note that the 1099 amount is reported to the IRS, but this does not necessarily mean, for example, that you have $1,000 worth of income when it says $1,000 on your 1099. This is because you may be entitled to deductions that reduce your amount of taxable income. By law, you are only required to receive a 1099 from those mystery shopping companies that have paid you $600 or more during the year. However, even if you don't receive a 1099, the income is still reportable.

A bit of good news is that you do not have taxes withheld from each payment you receive for doing your shops. So if you earn $40 for a shop, you don't receive a check for $25 after withholding of taxes. The bad news is that you are responsible for paying all of your own social security taxes at year-end, if you show a profit, which are normally split between you and your employer. Also, you may need to pay quarterly estimated income taxes (your tax advisor can figure this out for you). But these are not additional taxes, they are the taxes you would have paid over the course of the year anyway.

Even better news is that as someone who is self-employed, there are many deductions available to you, that are not possible for someone who is employed. Many shoppers get confused and think that they have to be "a business" to get deductions. Guess what? In the eyes of the IRS, as an independent contractor, you *are* a business. So you reap the benefits. For example, when someone burns through their gas each day commuting to work, it is money they generally do not get to deduct—you probably can.

Here is a list of some of the possible deductions you may be entitled to:

- mileage (if not reimbursed), or a percentage of your car's use for your mystery shopping work (this can include your car payment, repairs, maintenance)

- parking and tolls (if not reimbursed)

- business use of your home (a percentage of your rent or mortgage payment plus all utilities and insurance)

- telephone—cost of a second line, voicemail, phone calls (local and long distance related to your work)

- internet access—part or all of your dial-up ISP or high-speed internet monthly service charge

- postage (if not reimbursed)

- office equipment and supplies—this can include a percentage of the cost of the item for the amount that you use it in your mystery shopping work.

- Items such as a computer, fax, scanner, printer, digital camera, calculator, answering machine, file cabinet, a desk and chair, those expensive laser and fax toner cartridges, paper, paper clips, etc., all could be at least partially tax deductible to you.

You and your tax advisor can likely think of other deductions to which you would be entitled, but I just wanted to give you a good idea of what was possible. Notice how this is another way that you enhance your standard of living because the government, through tax deductions, helps subsidize your housing cost, equipment, car costs, and more. That digital camera you wanted to buy to take pictures of the kids, or to use on your next vacation, is now likely to be partly deductible for the amount you use it in your mystery shopping work.

What happens is that by allowing these deductions, you can substantially reduce the amount of profit you have as a mystery shopper for tax purposes. You may even proportionally pay a lot less income tax than if you were a W-2 employee because some of your costs that are tax-deductible are subsidized by the government. You may also be able to set up a special type of retirement account for yourself (such as a SEP-IRA). Such accounts are designed for self-employed people to allow you to put away a greater proportion of income for retirement based on how much profit you have from being self-employed. These accounts are also not available to W-2 employees and they can even further reduce your taxable income.

The end result is that each dollar you earn being self-employed could be worth a lot more to you than you think. Get yourself a good tax advisor if you don't have one already, or if you are a do-it-yourself type, get your hands on everything you can regarding self-employment and taxes.

Chapter Two: Notes/Questions

Chapter Three: Are You Legal?

Many shoppers assume since they are not a corporation and they are operating "undercover", that no one knows about what they do and they do not have to worry about local regulations. Wrong! Whenever you're self-employed, it's always a good idea to check with your local authorities to make sure you are not violating any regulations. Since you are working out of your home, you want to make sure that there is no issue with zoning laws or even with your home owner's association (if you have one) regarding this use of your home.

When I lived in Southern California, it's a given that lots of people have home-based businesses or telecommute and work out of their home. It's actually encouraged—one less commuter on the crowded freeways. You can't look at a home or apartment over one bedroom and not have the agent tell you how a particular room will "make a wonderful home office". In other parts of the country, there may be some 100-year old zoning law on the books that you need to be aware of. Since you are not operating a business with employees that is in any way visible to your neighbors, or could possibly interfere with their daily living, it's likely not an issue. Still, it never hurts to be sure.

Also be certain that you do not need any kind of business permit or occupational license such as a private investigator license to do mystery shopping work. In California, the Business and Professions code, section 7522, specifically lists someone who does mystery shopping work as exempt from private investigator laws. It excludes:

> "A person or business engaged in conducting objective observations of consumer purchases of products or services in the public environments of a business establishment by the use of a pre-established questionnaire, provided that person or business entity does not engage in any other activity that requires licensure pursuant to this chapter. The questionnaire may include objective comments."

I have heard however, that it is possible a state may require a private investigator license for mystery shopping work. Nevada does. So check on the rules in your state to know the facts and what would be required if you do need one. Do not rely on a mystery shopping company or scheduler to know this information. As an independent contractor, it's your responsibility to know the applicable laws. Plus, the addition of audio and video mystery shops to the assignment types now being done by mystery shoppers, may be considered to be beyond the scope of traditional work in that field by some jurisdictions.

A helpful web site I found with links regarding the private investigator laws in each state is www.crimetime.com/licensing.htm.

And if you do need a license, you shouldn't let this stop you from doing mystery shopping. Many businesses and professions require licenses, and if you take this work seriously and learn how to regularly generate assignments for yourself, you will make far more on an annual basis than the license cost. Besides, in most cases it is tax deductible (check with your tax advisor)!

Chapter Three: Notes/Questions

Chapter Four: So What Could I Really Be Earning?

If there is a pretty good demand for shoppers in your area, it is entirely possible to make up to $1,000 in a month's time in actual cash and freebies depending upon the types of shops you do with a "full-time" effort. You also may be able to even double that figure to as much as $2,000 in a month's time in major markets, or reach it more regularly, by taking on video and audio mystery shopping work. This is discussed in chapter twelve *Video Mystery Shopping.*

Other income boosters focus on complementary assignments such as report editing available to you as a more established shopper (see chapter nine *How To Maximize Your Income As A Mystery Shopper By Standing Out From The Crowd*) and scheduling work (see chapter ten *The Brass Ring: Scheduling)*—a very experienced independent scheduler can make as much as $2,500 a month! The more types of work you get involved with, the higher your income will be.

Of course, if you are in a rural area, don't count on reaching the upper ends of these income figures on shops alone, because the number of possible businesses in your area available to be shopped is much smaller. On the other hand, your cost of living is likely a lot lower too. Then again, I have seen a lot of desperate requests for shoppers in more remote areas of Northern California that almost made me want to drive a few hundred miles because the pay was so good (well, maybe if they also paid for mileage). If you live in or on the outskirts of a major city, you should do very well with the right amount of effort. One of my former coaching clients, D.S. in Duluth, Georgia (name withheld at her request, written testimonial on file), earned $1,980 in January, 2002, and that's without any video mystery shopping, scheduling or other work!

Despite what you may have heard, overall demand for mystery shoppers is great as companies realize the importance of staying competitive and providing a positive customer experience. You can work almost every day if you want to—if you get the word out about yourself properly, get a reputation for being reliable, are able to jump in at the last minute and do solid, professional work.

If you figure an average of $25 earned per shop in cash and/or freebies, this would mean if you just do strictly "traditional" mystery shopping, you need to do 40 shops per month to earn $1,000. For example, this could break down to an average of one a day for 30 days/two a day for 10 days, or two a day for 20 days. For the "one a day" schedule, figure that in the 10 cases where you need to do a second shop per day to hit your 40 shops per month goal, those could be restaurant shops. You wouldn't mind eating out in restaurants 10 times during the month would you? If you also did higher-paying audio and video shops, assuming an average of $50 for those, you could do just 25 shops and earn the same $1,000 (15 audio/video shops and 10 regular shops).

Generally, to keep the quality of your shops high, I do not recommend doing more than two or three complex shops in a day (although I have done four or five in a day on an emergency basis for high pay).

And when I say "full-time", I mean you are willing to do a shop or more a day, but a shop could take a half hour, a detailed, narrative report an hour, plus your travel time. This means you might have to work two hours a day, or maybe up to four hours a day to do two shops (timing varies by the shop type and your level of experience). I like that definition of full-time versus the standard eight hours or more most people think of! This gives full-time a whole new meaning!

Or if your goals are a bit more modest and you just want to earn some extra money (but more than you are making now), you can easily make $400 to $500 per month in actual cash and freebies without working weekends or even every day! Again, figure at an average of $25 per traditional mystery shopping job, you need 16 jobs to make $400 cash (or just 8 shops if they were audio/video at $50 apiece). Suppose you wanted to make $250 extra a month. Using a $25 average, that's just 10 traditional shops or 5 audio/video shops!

There also tends to be more work in the first few days of the month when new job orders come in to the schedulers, and at the end of the month when unfilled jobs run up against deadlines and shopper cancellations. Again, your actual earnings can be more or less depending upon the time you put in; where you live; and the type of shops you do. When you need more money, you can put in more time or change the types of shops you are willing to do.

If you have enough money to meet your needs in a particular month, you can kick back, go on vacation or work on whatever it is you are truly trying to do. I once took three weeks off while my Dad underwent surgery and I went to visit and help out in Florida. It was nice to have that freedom to drop everything and be where I was needed the most without having to beg anyone for time off.

When I came back, I wanted to get back into the swing of things and earn some money, so I took on nine jobs and earned $239.50 (all but $5 was cash) in eight days for an average of $29.94 per shop. If I kept that pace up for the month, I could have earned about $900. But I wanted to get back to my writing and coaching, and as one of my favorite live musical performers Eddie Money says in the song "It's Another Nice Day in L.A., *"I could get to the top but I don't want to work that hard"*. Besides I was about to go away for a long weekend with my husband and then back to Florida to visit my Dad again. But that's the beauty of it. <u>Make money when you want to on your terms, and don't when you have other things to do</u>.

So as you can see, there is more money to be made as a mystery shopper than you might have thought, and free items and services that can be paid for that will certainly stretch your budget. You'll also get paid for doing things you would do anyway, and/or have items paid for that you would have bought anyway. Plus, the tax effect of having the government subsidize your living expenses by making expenditures you have as a consumer or employee that were not tax deductible, or had limited deductibility, fully deductible against independent contractor income, your standard of living is enhanced as well.

So what's your earnings goal? Figure out where you want to be income-wise, how much time you are willing to devote to shops, see if you are willing to do the more complex shops and make a commitment to get there using the information in this book and acting on it.

It is easier to reach a particular earnings number when you calculate what it takes and then you can step up or cut back on your efforts as I do. It's just like I calculated it in this chapter. Take what you expect to be your average pay per shop (should be $20-$25 at least in most cases) and divide it into what you want your total income to be for the month. If the number of shops sounds high, you have some work to do, assuming your goal is realistic given your time and market. If it sounds good, go for it, and then raise the bar a little next month and see if you can surprise yourself with how much you can make!

Chapter Four: Notes/Questions

Chapter Five: Mystery Shopper Income Drainers

Earning top money as a mystery shopper is as much to do with doing everything right, as it is with avoiding mistakes. See if you recognize any of your habits in these 9 income drainers and then take steps to plug up the leaks in your mystery shopper income (sorry, it was there, I had to use it).

1. Taking On Shops That Are Too Far Away

When someone is a beginning mystery shopper, I advise them to consider assignments that are out of their typical geographic area to get experience and their foot in the door. But if you've got experience, you should no longer be driving all over the place.

You need to keep in mind your gas mileage and how much it costs you to travel a certain distance. It's easy to forget the economics of travel when you get a shop assignment. You hate to turn down work of any kind. Plus, you also start to get in the habit of sending in for anything in your area. You see your city mentioned in a job lead posting and you instantly send in for the assignment—like a game show contestant ringing in to answer a question.

But take a step back and do the math. If you have to drive 25 miles (and I certainly don't recommend this distance in many markets) to an assignment without reimbursement for mileage (but mileage may be tax deductible to you—check with your tax advisor), and you have a gas-guzzling SUV that gets 12 miles per gallon, you've gone through 4 gallons of gas round-trip. Gas prices vary across the country, but say that gallon cost you $3.00 (at the time of this writing). You've spent $12.00 in gas. The shop offers to pay $15. That means you earn $3.00 for the shop (not including the after-tax effect). Is that worth it?

Your time is a factor as well. When I lived in Southern California, you had to drive just about everywhere. Because of traffic and the sheer volume of cars on the road, it could take you quite awhile to get where you're going. You have to decide how much drive time that you could be using for other assignments, other work you do, or for living your life, you are willing to give up for each assignment.

If you are going to do shops that are farther away than would normally make sense from a cost and time perspective, don't be afraid to ask the company or scheduler offering that assignment for one or more additional shops to be completed in the same or a nearby area to make it worth your while. If you see they are desperate to get a particular assignment filled you can also try to ask for mileage reimbursement. Sometimes it works. I do this all the time. If you are known by the company or scheduler as a reliable shopper, they will be happy to accommodate you—one less assignment for which they need to find a shopper!

2. Too Much Narrative For Too Little Pay

Before you accept an assignment, you need to know honestly how much of it is narrative versus "yes or no" or very simple, one sentence answers being required. This way, you will know if the pay is worth the effort that is expected. Not all companies will pay the same for the same type of shop or level of effort. I have seen apartment shops, which are probably about the most complex type of shop, that had two pages of narrative that paid as little as $15, while others paid $20, $25, $30 or even up to $50. They all required the same amount of effort, which is why you have to learn what is reasonable so you don't get taken advantage of.

And make sure that "super easy shop" you're being pitched truly has minimal narrative. What is "very little narrative" from one person's point-of-view, can be a bit exaggerated at times. Do not hesitate to ask to see the shop forms before officially accepting the job.

3. <u>Any Shop That Pays Less Than $20</u>

You know the ones. Those fast food shops where you only get a free lunch. Or that same assignment might offer a reimbursement of $10 with a requirement to order a certain item, and you get to keep what's left so you net only $5 to $7 (not including the free food). That's not going to pay many bills.

Then there's the "fun" or "quick and easy" shop for $7 or $8 at a cell phone store or video store. If you live down the block from one of these great, if not....

Personally, now that I am very experienced, I won't do a shop that pays under $20 unless:

- It is right in my immediate neighborhood, or another one that I visit regularly anyway, and is a quick "yes or no" check-off form without a narrative.

- It is an opportunity to get experience with a new type of shop.

- It is an opportunity to get "in" with a new company for whom I want to work.

- There is also a reimbursed freebie as part of the deal that makes the overall value $20 or more (and it is something I want or would actually use).

- It is an easy, no-narrative, regularly-occurring shop in my immediate neighborhood, or another one I visit regularly, so my monthly income from the job is worthwhile. Plus once you repeat a shop, you'll likely start doing it faster.

- I can combine one or more easy jobs in the same stop, so my overall stop is worth $20 or more. The time you would normally spend in travel time is eliminated, making a multi-shop stop, even if each shop is lower-paying, more worthwhile.

- I can combine it with one or more merchandising assignments (for more Information, go to my web site at:

http://www.mysteryshoppercoach.com/merchandising.
html and consider getting a copy of my book *The
Quick And Easy Guide To Making Money As A
Merchandiser* available 24/7 at
http://www.mysteryshoppercoach.com/books.html.

Remember, the time spent doing a low-paying shop is
time you could be spending doing a high-paying shop.
Sure, sometimes you need the cash and have to take on
anything and everything, but when possible, use $20+ as
your target fee per shop (adjust this figure if necessary for
your market).

4. Poor Record Keeping

Do you keep careful track of which companies you need
to invoice versus those who send your pay automatically?
How about when your payments are due and which are
late so you can do follow-up? To be a top-earning
shopper you need to do many, many shops each month
and it's easy to lose track of such things if you are not
organized. See Chapter 8 *Are You Making Costly
Mistakes In Your Reporting And Post-Shop Activities?* for
how to handle this effectively.

While it doesn't happen that often, I also sometimes have
heard from shoppers about disputes regarding payment.
This can be another drain on your income while payment
is delayed. Even in this day of electronic record keeping
(and e-books of course), an electronic AND paper trail is
your best defense.

I recommend that when you get a new shop assignment, download any files immediately and save them in a file on your computer where you can find them again. Also print out that assignment e-mail and everything in these downloads—forms, guidelines, etc., for your file. It is also a very good practice to confirm back the assignment award in an e-mail upon receipt. These items will be your records that prove you were assigned the shop. They also provide proof of the instructions you were given for completing the shop in case any conflicts arise. It also never hurts to download files immediately to be sure that you do not have any problems doing so.

5. <u>Losing Money For Improper Reporting</u>

Your report is everything to the client and is the basis upon which you get paid. Don't cheat yourself out of getting the maximum fee for each assignment you complete. Watch report submission deadlines. Sure you know when your shop is due, but remember the shop deadline and report submission deadline can be two different dates that often conflict, making you think you have more time to submit the report than you do. For example, it's June 9th, your shop is due by June 12th and your report must be filed 24 hours after shop completion. You did the shop June 10th, which means your report is due June 11th even though your overall shop deadline gave you till June 12th.

Make sure you also file an accurate report and do not miss sections where comments or narrative is called for especially on what appears to be "an easy check-off form". When you know you have to write a page on your apartment shop, you won't miss that requirement. When a small instruction on the page says to give a comment for every "no" answer, that could be missed if you read the form in a rush.

6. <u>Waiting For Mystery Shopping Companies To Contact You</u>

Many books that have been published on mystery shopping advise you to apply to any and all mystery shopping companies left and right. I recently saw someone proudly post on a message board that she had applied to over 200 companies and got a shop assignment. If I spent my time applying to 200 companies, I wouldn't be so thrilled that I got "a" shop. I also hear from shoppers all the time who have applied to lots of companies and are wondering why they hardly ever get an assignment from them (if they get one at all).

I disagree with the "apply to hundreds of companies" approach because the odds of a particular company having an assignment in your area, and then bothering to go through their database to find you is slim. The larger, and many of the better, mystery shopping companies outsource the booking of their mystery shopping jobs. This makes sense. Why should a company bother trying to find a shopper for a particular assignment—especially on short notice—when they can pass along whole batches of jobs ordered by their clients to the independent schedulers who handle that aspect of things for them? And even when they do handle assignment bookings in-house, it's better to apply in response to actual job leads they post in one of many places on the internet.

Think of a "real world" job search. If you just apply to companies all over the place without any experience, or knowing if they even have any job openings, it's going to be a fruitless effort. Once you are awarded an assignment applied for in this fashion, you are in the company scheduler's database as a proven shopper who they are familiar with—quite a difference!

Keep in mind, you want to spend your time actually doing assignments (where you earn money) and not spend your time searching for, and trying to land assignments (where you do not earn money). Time spent looking for work is time spent not working! **There is only one time when you should apply directly to a company's web site, to learn the secret, go to: http://www.mysteryshoppercoach.com/secretsites.ht ml.**

7. Checking Leads On Too Many Mystery Shopping Companies' Web Sites

This is directly related to having applied to too many mystery shopping companies in the first place. Personally, unless it is a company I regularly do work with (and in those cases, they are almost always contacting me first anyway), I tend to just keep up with the companies that will e-mail me when they have an assignment in my area with the specific job in the message, or at minimum, a notification that new assignments in my area are posted on their web site to check out. Also be aware that some web sites are sophisticated enough to contact you with jobs that really are in your area, while others will contact you if it is anywhere in your state. When I lived in California, it was annoying and a waste of time to get an e-mail for an assignment that is 600 miles away. But that was also the price you pay for knowing that there is a job you are interested in just five miles away.

8. Checking Leads On Too Many Mystery Shopping Boards/Groups

Just like in #7 above, it is easy to get to be a message board junkie. You sign up for what seems like every group out there on Topica, Delphi and Yahoo thinking "aha—I've got all my bases covered!" Then you're deluged with e-mails, or go on the boards to check for work (an exhausting process in itself) and find that most of the same jobs are listed everywhere.

That's not a surprise, because companies rarely list their available jobs directly with a lead board—schedulers for these companies who are very good and very active do, or independent schedulers from companies like Kern do. Their goal is to get the word out and they don't want to leave any stone unturned. Also, unless you are on a state or country-specific board or list, you are going to see messages for everywhere and you don't shop everywhere. Even if you ignore these postings, you've still got to scan through them.

What's the better way to hear about these jobs? See Chapter Six: *The Key To Top Mystery Shopper Earnings* for more details on this.

9. Being Afraid To Say "No"

You get a call from company A and they want you to do a shop for them, but you aren't wild about taking it on. Last time you worked with them, they gave you an employee to target for your apartment shop that never picked up the phone so it took forever to complete the job. Their form also kept doing crazy things to your computer so it took you longer than usual to complete your report. Finally, they paid $5 less than all your other apartment shop companies and took 60 days to pay. No wonder you're not excited about the project!

Don't be afraid to stop accepting assignments from companies that you don't enjoy working with or are slow to pay. For example, I did a lot of apartment shops, and I stopped working with one company in my market area that was a lot like what I just described to deal with. Give them the heave-ho. Life is too short, and there are too many other companies to work with.

Chapter Five: Notes/Questions

Chapter Six: The Key To Top Mystery Shopper Earnings

If you aren't already working with independent schedulers (and lots of them), you're missing out on the key to top earnings as a mystery shopper—getting known by those who control the big batches of jobs.   If you are working with them, you may not be in touch with as many as you should be—giving emphasis to the mystery shopping companies themselves (a mistake in most cases). You also simply may not be getting all you can out of these valuable contacts.

For those of you who don't know, such schedulers are the middlemen, (or should I say "middlewomen" since most that I have come across are female) of the mystery shopping industry. They end up handling job assignments for many of the larger, and better, mystery shopping companies out there. Even if you apply directly with a mystery shopping company and are in their database, the odds of you ever hearing from them for a job are not high in most situations.

Here's a case in point. I registered through the web site of a mystery shopping company and have done many, many shops for them. However, I have never, ever been contacted directly by them for an assignment. Every single bit of work has come through independent schedulers who book shops for them. Had I been waiting for this company to contact me for a job, I would still be waiting. Instead, I was making money!

By the same token, isn't it better use of your time to get known by several independent schedulers who will be handling multiple assignments for all different companies on an ongoing basis, than having to find a job here from company A and a job there from company B? Trust me, this is the fastest way to get your shopping jobs and more importantly, <u>keep getting shopping assignments coming to you</u>!

Plus, once you make contact with several schedulers, they will add you to their database as an active shopper in your area, and e-mail you job leads for their assignments (that are actually in your area so you don't have to wade through all different state headings) usually before, or at least simultaneously, with postings on the job lead boards. Sometimes, schedulers will even call you or e-mail you personally to ask you if you would like a particular job once you get well-known by them and have proven yourself. I am fortunate to now be in this category. As a reader of this book, you will be too!

Again, in case you haven't worked with schedulers before, please note that you don't have to pay anything to them for a job. They are compensated by the mystery shopping company for matching you up with one of their assignments.

So how do you reach the independent schedulers? They regularly post job leads to various shopper message boards that are updated on the internet—sometimes many times a day as new job leads come in. You can identify a scheduler by their signature at the end of the posting which will say "Jane Doe for 123 Scheduling".

Two of the biggest scheduling companies use lots of schedulers or "agents"—Palm Scheduling and Kern Scheduling. Their schedulers use PSS and KSS or IscheduleShop in their e-mail addresses, respectively. There are also some mystery shopping companies who have their own schedulers that focus exclusively on their jobs. A company who is aggressive enough to post jobs with their own schedulers is worth knowing.

Check out the following and decide which two or three serve your needs the best. You are looking to make scheduler contacts (and continue to make them). Remember, you don't need to be involved with every board out there because the schedulers will post the same job leads all over. The bulk of my work came from being "connected" with schedulers. Once I felt I had gotten connected with all the major schedulers who could help with assignments in my area, I just kept tabs on these lead resources in case someone new popped up to cover my bases.

If you are one of my readers from Canada or another country outside the United States, I will note which sources will apply specifically to you. By going onto a country-specific version of Yahoo!®, like Yahoo Canada, you can likely turn up other lead boards and groups not mentioned here.

Some of my favorites are Yahoo! Groups. These are all discussion groups catering to those looking for leads for mystery shopping assignments and to connect with schedulers. Most of them require that you be approved to join the group. Not a big deal really, just follow the instructions and you'll be added—they just want to avoid spammers or those who aren't really interested in the topic at hand that will cause trouble.

Simply go to the main Yahoo!® Groups page at: http://groups.yahoo.com. Then type in the name(s) of the group(s) you wish to join, one by one. Here are several top ones:

- mysteryshoppingbyncpms

- mystery-shopper

- mystery-shops

- mysteryshopspay45

- mystery_shoppers_usa

- restaurantbarms

- secret-shopper

- lots-o-funms

This will bring you to each group's main page where you can click on "join this group" and be added instantly, or after being approved.

Depending on the volume of messages, or how often you tend to see listings in your area in their postings, you can either select individual delivery of e-mails to get access to postings fastest (but you will have a bunch of e-mails in your in-box, or adjust the setting for e-mail delivery to digest form for very active group (downside is you may miss out on assignments when you only get one e-mail a day). If you don't mind having a bunch of e-mails, you can quickly scan the headings to see what isn't appropriate and hit "delete" as you read subject lines that clearly you have no interest in. In the future, you won't have to check these resources as often because you'll be known and in all the key company and individual schedulers databases. It will also give you a good idea in the beginning of the various kinds of shops that come up, and what they tend to pay and require so you can decide what you want to try for.

If you subscribe to Delphi newsgroups (similar to Yahoo!® Groups) there are several devoted to mystery shopping. Just go to www.delphiforums.com and enter the topic "mystery shopping" to get a list of newsgroups that are available. Some are geared to a particular state, some to just offering leads, and others to offering information and assistance. Canadian shoppers—there is a Delphi group just for you located at http://forums.delphiforums.com/canshoppers/start. Check through the various offerings and see if any of them are of interest to you. But pick a couple of favorites and that's it!

Topica has a very good mailing list as well at: http://www.topica.com/lists/msopenings

The Mystery Shoppers Providers Association (MSPA), a trade association for businesses who offer mystery shopping services also has a section that sometimes has leads for shoppers—both in the U.S., as well as Canada, Europe and other countries. Go to www.mysteryshop.org/shoppers, you'll be taken to a page where you can sort your search by your location, type of assignment you are looking for, etc. There is also a board for networking with other mystery shoppers. By the way, don't worry about the certifications they talk about—you don't need them!

In addition to working with the resources I have listed above, You'll want to get into the shopper databases of the two largest scheduling companies—Kern Scheduling Services and Palm Scheduling Services. Some changes have occurred recently with both of these companies that is important to understand in working with them. Kern and Palm have transitioned many of their jobs over to automated systems that have pros and cons for mystery shoppers. On the plus side, if you are in the overall database for each of these companies, you'll theoretically be "known" to each of their schedulers when the system sends out e-mails for their job assignments without worrying that you've missed somebody. Plus, when you want to take the initiative and look for jobs on your own for some reason (remember your goal is to spend as little time looking for work as possible—let the leads come to you), or if you are traveling (see Chapter Nine for more on this), you can see what's doing in a particular area.

On the negative side, these automated systems take some of the personal contact out of your interaction with a mystery shopping company and/or scheduler, so it's harder to get known and not just be one person in a sea of mystery shoppers. These new systems also tend to provide rankings of shoppers through a formula so higher-ranked shoppers get preference for an assignment (this can be a pro or a con depending how you are ranked and what goes into the rating system).

Be very careful with these automated systems to put down all applicable areas to be sure you are not left out of any prime assignments that happen to be on the border of your city or share an area code.

To get into the Kern Scheduling Services database, go to: http://www.kernscheduling.com.

To get into the Palm Scheduling Services database, go to: www.palmschedulingservices.com.

There are also many sites which I call "pay for leads" sites that offer shoppers the opportunity to register for an annual fee or lifetime fee, and then provide any or all of the following services: they deliver shop assignment leads to you by e-mail from the schedulers who post jobs to their sites; let companies and schedulers find you via a profile; and allow you to search for shops on their site. I've personally put two of these services to the test and generally find they could be of value for some shoppers—especially if you combine the methods for marketing yourself to schedulers in this book with the additional lead contacts you'll make through these services. Yet, you also need to be careful, as there are certainly many other sites out there which are requiring payment that are nothing but scams. Overall, do not in any way feel that it is necessary to sign up for a "pay for leads" site, as you can certainly get by without signing up for these services since you are already empowered by the knowledge in this book.

Tip: *If you haven't already thought of this, consider adding a free e-mail address account such as those available from Yahoo®! for your newsgroup or newsletter correspondence. Not for your schedulers and company contacts, since you want those going to your primary, professional e-mail address. Use this secondary freebie e-mail address to subscribe to newsgroups or newsletters so you can read these at your leisure. Plus if you sign-up for several, they will not clutter up your main e-mail address where those money-generating e-mail messages are coming in. If you find a newsgroup is turning into a great source of leads for you and they have a subscribe option, you can always change the e-mail address that their messages are delivered to over to your primary address.*

Overall, you'll find that using two or three favorites as your primary lead resources may be all you need to get started. In the beginning though, you'll likely want to check several leads resources to make sure you have your bases covered and until you see which ones are the best fits for you. You also may need to do more searching among the resources like the MSPA to find shops if you live in a less-populated area.

Once you make contact with several schedulers, they will add you to their databases as an active shopper in your area, and e-mail you job leads for their assignments usually before, or at least simultaneously, with postings on the job lead boards. Sometimes, schedulers will even call you or e-mail you personally to ask you if you would like a particular job once you get well-known by them and have proven yourself. I was fortunate to get into this category. As a reader of this book, you too will be soon!

This is another reason why you don't need to get obsessed with reviewing dozens of lead boards or applying to hundreds of companies. Now while I believe connecting with schedulers is optimal for the reasons I have given, I know shoppers get antsy about networking, or do not always have timely e-mail access to jump on the latest shopper opportunities that the schedulers they are connected with send their way. Also many shoppers like to do jobs when they travel, and want easy access to assignments in the area to which they will be heading.

So now I'll share with you a secret. **There is one type of company, and only one that makes sense to apply to directly, as you have some spare time. To learn the secret of the only mystery shopping web sites you should ever apply to directly, go to http://www.mysteryshoppercoach.com/secretsites.html**

Chapter Six: Notes/Questions

Chapter Seven: Getting The Most Out Of Working With Schedulers

Let's go back to the basics for a moment, so you can make sure you're not making a mistake on the easy stuff. When you get your e-mail updates from a Yahoo!® Group, Kern or Palm Scheduling, or an independent scheduler, review them right away. And "right away" on the internet, in case you haven't realized it, is not hours later or the next day—it is often measured in minutes. The most desirable assignments go fast! To save time, just scan the headings for your state or any that say "shoppers needed in many states". If you live in California, you are not doing a shop in South Carolina tomorrow in all likelihood, so don't bother reading about the assignment. (I know, sometimes out of curiosity you peek at that lead for Oshkosh when you live in Florida—forget it, there's no mileage reimbursement)!

As you see an assignment that is in your area, read the message carefully to see what specific cities jobs are in, details about the assignment like pay and due date, what is required, and most importantly, how to respond. Be sure you do what the scheduler asks to have the best shot of getting the job or to at least be considered for future jobs.

If they say to e-mail them with the city of the job in the heading, do it. If they say call, do it. If they ask you to supply certain information about yourself, do it. If they tell you they are posting for a friend and you must e-mail their friend and not them, *absolutely do it*. (Don't you hate it when you get e-mail from a familiar mystery shopping contact and then you realize it's for someone else, so you have to be careful not to hit "reply" so you don't annoy anyone)? The ability to follow instructions is an important part of being a good shopper—demonstrate this by following them in applying for the assignment. If you can't follow instructions to get the job, why should you get the job?

You have two goals in responding to job leads posted by the schedulers:

- To get the job you are applying for; and

- To get in their database for direct e-mail notification of future assignments.

So how do you get in with that scheduler? Yes, if at first you don't succeed, try, try again! I found you just had to be persistent and keep answering lead board postings by the schedulers and the job assignments started happening. I also started getting my first trickle and then a rush of scheduler e-mails letting me know about jobs. Aha! <u>That's what I wanted—jobs coming to me, rather than me having to go look for them</u>. I'll admit there's one or two schedulers that I just was not been able to break in with. I got an "it's nothing personal, but you were five seconds late in responding to this job posting, so it went to another shopper e-mail" every time. But keep trying, you'll break through to them one of these days. In fact, hold out for their desperation. When they just can't get that assignment booked and have to offer $50 for the $20 job, that's when you'll get even (just kidding).

Actually, don't be afraid to add little polite notations in your responses to schedulers' job postings that you've been trying to work together for awhile with no luck and restating your qualifications. I have actually appealed to some schedulers that then "threw me a bone". I got in, and we worked together after that.

Now it is true that the higher level of automation among some of the big scheduling companies is making it more difficult to use these more personal techniques to stand out. Still there are many mystery shopping companies and schedulers who directly review their e-mails for shop leads where these points will work. Plus, be observant, when you get an e-mail from a scheduler that is non-automated in relation to some aspect of your assignment (usually after it is awarded or if you write in with a question on an assignment), start keeping track of their actual e-mail addresses, so you can e-mail them as a "human" when it is appropriate to maintain that personal touch.

By the way, even as an experienced shopper, if your work has all been for a particular type of shop, it is a great idea to diversify yourself as they say in investing. You should have experience in retail, restaurant and/or fast food and service categories (automotive, apartments, banking, fitness centers for example), as well as the new technology-based shops (audio and video). It shows that you can handle all types of observations—quick checklists, lengthy narratives and those that involved the use of technology. And the better you look on paper to a scheduler and they realize that you will be the shopper they love to give assignments to, the more jobs you'll get on a steady basis and your income will show the difference!

Plus, if you make sure you are diversified into service category shops and audio/video shops—these are generally going to pay the most and demonstrate that you are a higher caliber shopper, so try to focus on them. If you are serious about earning as much as possible doing mystery shopping work, that's where the money is. Besides, you will also get your best chance of securing other work, like report editing, by showing what you can do on those narrative sections.

In the Resource Section, I have included the response letter I used and tweaked to fit the particular job assignment for which I was trying. You should review it and then create one in your own voice and style. Essentially, you should have the following components in addition to any specifics the scheduler has asked for:

- put the city, state and type of shop in the subject section of your e-mail (unless other instructions for response are given).

- indicate the job you are contacting the scheduler about (type, city, state, due date) and how you heard about it.

- **this is the most important point right here—** <u>have a line saying that if this assignment is no longer available, please add you to their database for future jobs</u>. A good scheduler often will do it automatically, but don't assume it to be the case.

Schedulers always need to know about new, available, experienced people, and you will hear from them down the line, if not immediately.

- briefly touch upon your mystery shopper experience, and any related experience you have that addresses what makes you a good shopper. For myself, it was my prior marketing and market research experience and the fact that I was in retailing and financial services (since many shops are available in these industries). Also mention some companies you regularly work with and types of shops you specialize in (do not ever name specific clients for these shops (i.e. Joe's gym).

- list when you are generally available to work and if your hours are flexible, if you are available weekdays, weekends or both, etc.

- include some of your qualities that make you a good shopper, such as your ability to meet deadlines, that you pay close attention to details, you are PC literate, etc.

- provide the cities/towns you will shop in (knowing that the distance is reasonable given your time and that you are not reimbursed for gas/mileage).

- thank the scheduler for their time and provide all your key contact information in a block of type— name, e-mail address, address, phone number and fax number or signature file if your e-mail program allows you to do so.

By the way, do all the companies and schedulers you work with know your coverage area? It should be included in every e-mail response you send out. Don't assume because you filled it out once on a company's web site or you are in a scheduler's database, that they are going to bother to look through it and make the connection that they can offer you—reliable, professional shopper that they love—several assignments. Politely put it in front of them. See the Resource Section for my sample e-mail correspondence for how I handle this.

Chapter Seven: Notes/Questions

Chapter Eight: Are You Making Costly Mistakes In Your Reporting And Post-Shop Activities?

The most important part of your shop isn't the shop itself, it's the report. Sure you need to make observations and follow instructions, but it is the report that goes to the mystery shopping company, scheduler (sometimes) and ultimately, the client. Also, even if you are an ace on reporting, maybe you are not using your report submission as the opportunity to subtly market yourself and stand out from the crowd that it is. As I mentioned earlier, if you're not well-organized you could be letting money you've earned slip through your fingers. Make sure you're handling Reporting, Report Submission and the Post-Reporting Period correctly and to your advantage.

1. Reporting

Carefully fill out the shop forms and if possible, put any longer narratives on a separate Microsoft® Word (or a plain text) document and just state "see attached document for narrative details". I have found that many shopping companies' forms are not geared well towards the narrative portion and I am not going to spend hours dealing with their software bugs.

Review your forms for obvious grammatical errors, accuracy and misspellings (use your spell check) and overuse of the same words. Keep a thesaurus or dictionary handy if you must so you don't bore the client to tears reading your report. Plus, watch for potential conflicts between what you said in answering a question versus what is in your narrative. If you checked off "no" when asked if you would buy a car from this dealer, but later in the narrative say how well they treated you and the good deal they gave you, that would not make sense.

You should also make sure you just give factual answers and save any opinions or suggestions until the end of the report if asked for them. I know, I know, sometimes it is so tempting to say what the employee should be doing, but save it unless the company specifically asks for such feedback. Remember, you are a researcher, and researchers report facts. Again, be sure that the report is being submitted within the allotted time after the shop has been completed even if the deadline is a few days away. It is rare for a mystery shopping company to accept a report that has been filed more than 24 to 48 hours after the shop took place. If you will be e-mailing your report, be sure to follow any instructions about naming your saved file for the company's convenience.

2. Report Submission

Review the guidelines and any instructions from either the scheduler or mystery shopping company to be sure that you properly submit your report. An incomplete report may not be accepted, or your payment may be reduced. Include any requested documents such as receipts (obviously very important for retail, airport or restaurant shops where you are going to be reimbursed), business cards, apartment floor plans, etc.

Again, this may be basic, but especially when you do a lot of shops, it is easy to start assuming you "know the drill" and overlook the way company A wants something versus the way company B wants it. You also could miss some new instruction for report filing since the last time you did a shop for them. I've shopped just about every location of a gym in my area that was within reasonable distance to me, and I know the shop and submission process by heart. Yet, I always take the time to download the latest file and review it because they have made subtle changes from time-to-time like who the report goes to via e-mail (an important thing to know)!

Use the right method of submission and be certain that the method you choose does not result in a reduced fee if at all possible (i.e. faxing vs. e-mail). If you are e-mailing, make sure that you have attached your report as a file (it's easy to forget if you rush or are in the middle of submitting several reports), and send the report to the e-mail address you have been instructed to use (not your scheduler's unless they have specifically requested to receive a copy). Put something like "Joe's XYZ Shop, Anywhere, CA Complete" as the subject line and a short note (see the Resource Section for a sample).

Essentially you want to accomplish the following with this note:

- repeat which report is included;

- tell the company to please contact you if they have any questions or problem opening the attachment;

- state that you would appreciate confirmation that the report has been received; and

- indicate you enjoyed working with the company, appreciated the opportunity and hope to do so again soon.

Conclude your message by signing off with your contact information block or signature.

If your scheduler has not requested to receive a copy of your report submission, send him or her an e-mail letting them know that the report has been completed and sent to the contact at the e-mail address they instructed you to use. Also mention that you enjoyed working with them and hope to do so again soon. If this is the first time you are working with the particular scheduler, remind them to please include you in their database and e-mails of assignments with which they need help. Sign off with your contact block/signature. (There is also a sample of this letter in the Resource Section for your convenience).

Taking the little bit of extra time to send e-mail correspondence like this is good business etiquette— much like when you write a thank you note for a job interview. Not everyone does it, and it helps you look professional and stand out in a positive way for future assignment consideration. You'd be surprised how often your "my report's finished/thanks for the job" e-mail arrives in that scheduler's "in-box" just as they have a rush job or a cancellation from another shopper. And guess who gets the job? You—the professional shopper who bothered to take a few extra minutes to make themselves stand out from the crowd!

3. Post-Reporting Period

Print out a copy of your report, your cover e-mail or fax. Place that along with any receipts, business cards or other materials from the shop in the file you have created just for that mystery shopping company in case they did not get your report, or you need back-up materials to help with questions from the mystery shopping company or client later on. Of course, also include in the file, as I mentioned earlier, a copy of your assignment award confirmation, assignment guidelines and e-mail confirmation of the assignment award back to the scheduler or company.

Keep these items until you are paid for the shop (and the check clears if it is the first time you have worked with a particular company). Then you can throw out the report if you like. I usually save at least a sample of a report for each type of shop I do for future reference.

Next, you should log the shop information into your records so you will know about payment due dates; and can keep track of how much you are earning for the month and when you can do the shop again (if there are restrictions). E-mail me at Melanie@mysteryshoppercoach.com for a free copy of my cool Excel spreadsheet that tracks all of the necessary information along with a running total of your monthly earnings.

If the company you are working with requires you to send an invoice or some other type of payroll form at the end of the month for all the shops you have completed for them (fill in the form as you go during the month to save time and so you don't forget any shops), put a note on your calendar to remind you to send it in so you get paid promptly.

I also recommend putting a note in your calendar as to when you should receive your payment by based on their stated guidelines. If a week past that date goes by without your receiving a payment, drop a polite e-mail, or make a polite phone call to the mystery shopping company's office (not your scheduler), to verify the status—sometimes records fall through the cracks. When you receive the payment, make a note in your records or on my information sheet.

Suppose the worst-case scenario happens and you are having problems getting paid? What do you do to get what's coming to you?

Contact the company again, still politely, but a little firmer this time. Determine what the issue is and get a definite commitment as to when a check will be received (note the date, time and who you spoke with in your records). If you still don't get your check as promised, make one more contact and ask for a supervisor or owner (if it's a small company). Mention that you "have enjoyed working for them but their payment is now seriously overdue". Add that "you cannot do any more work for them until you receive payment for the work you have done". Close with the point that you "believed you were working with a quality company, and wanted to resolve this amicably, but if you don't receive your check within the next week, you will have no choice but to contact The Better Business Bureau and register a complaint against their business" (again note date, time, person spoken with).

The last call should really do it, but if not, follow-up on your promise to contact The Better Business Bureau (www.bbb.org) in your local area and file that complaint.

Suppose the issue is non-payment or reduced payment because of an issue with your report? Here's where the paper trail we just discussed helps, even in this electronic age.

Provide documentation to the company along with a polite, but firm (not nasty) e-mail or letter explaining why you are correct about the deadline, the way you conducted the shop, etc., keeping a copy for yourself. If this doesn't work, you can contact the Better Business Bureau and post about the experience tactfully in a forum to warn others.

Again, it is rare to have a non-payment issue in mystery shopping, but now you'll know what to do and what kinds of records to keep to win your claim.

Chapter Eight: Notes/Questions

Chapter Nine: How To Maximize Your Income As A Mystery Shopper By Standing Out From The Crowd

Based upon my experience, here are 10 ways that you can earn the most from your mystery shopping work.

1. Be a Professional

As you've already seen, I feel it is very important to have proper e-mail correspondence that can be used in your dealings with schedulers or mystery shopping contacts. You should create some sample e-mails that cover the following situations:

- Sample Response to a Job Lead Posting

- "Keep Me in Mind" Response (for when you don't get the job)

- "Assignment Acknowledgement" (for when you do get the job)

- "Thank You for the Assignment" (for your scheduler after you have completed the job)

- Report Submission Message (for your mystery shopping contact)

- Touching Base (when you want to remind schedulers or mystery shopping companies you work with of your availability)

These are small touches, but they go a long way in making you memorable to schedulers and portraying yourself as a professional mystery shopper that can be counted upon to do the job in a quality manner. See the Resource Section for some sample letters that you can adapt to your own style.

You can further demonstrate your professionalism by doing assignments correctly, handing in well-written reports and, above all, getting the assignment done and handed in on time. If you are having trouble completing your assignment after doing everything possible to attempt the shop as instructed, do not hesitate to ask the mystery shopping company for additional assistance and guidance. If you are not going to meet the deadline for an assignment, let the company and your scheduler know as soon as possible, to see if an extension is possible, or in case they need to make arrangements to give the job to another shopper who can complete the job in time. The same holds true if you are not going to be able to do a shop at all—you get sick, your car dies, you are called out of town, etc. Give both your scheduler and the mystery shopping company as much notice as possible to re-assign the shop.

While it is assumed that if you accept an assignment, you will complete it, life happens and everyone understands (as long as you rarely cancel out on a shop because then you could end up canceling yourself out of future assignments for good). Giving advance notice immediately will be respected and not knock you out of consideration for the future. That said, always try to do your shops well-ahead of the deadline, so the chances that life will interfere will be a lot lower.

I once was supposed to do an oil change shop with my husband's Mitsubishi® and wouldn't you know it, the morning I was supposed to go for the shop, the car would not start. The car eventually had to be towed to the repair shop and needed a new starter. I immediately contacted my scheduler and let her know what had happened. Not only did she thank me for letting her know so quickly, she was able to work with me to extend the deadline for the shop so I was still able to do the assignment.

Here's a word about kids and being a professional. If you are a stay-at-home Mom or Dad, you might be wondering if it's okay to bring your kids along on shops. My advice would be to bring them along if you need to if the kids really are well-behaved. This is a "work-at-home "career" and one of the benefits is the flexibility it can offer you in caring for, and spending time with your kids.

Keep in mind though, part of portraying yourself as a professional mystery shopper is to be focused on your assignment. Since you are being paid to make detailed observations, your ability to do your very best may be compromised if little Joey is running amuck and you are distracted. Some companies also may not permit your children coming along on a particular assignment. Of course in some cases, having a child (or access to one) is helpful or even necessary in order to be able to do an assignment—a toy store shop, a day care center, the babysitting facility at a gym, etc. So overall, use your judgement and be sure to note if an assignment does not permit a child to be taken along. If you are not sure, always ask!

2. Group Assignments Together

This idea is very important for time management so that you can get the most shops in within the time you have to devote to the work each week. Plus, it is key if you do retail shops which often take place in a local mall or major strip center. It is a waste of your time and gas to make a trip for one shop and then have to go back to the same location for another one, and perhaps another one. While scheduling may not always permit, do your best to not do a solo shop in such a location.

Combining assignments may also make a lower paying shop more attractive if it is quick and you can do it with one or two other ones on the same trip. If you can do three $7 to $12 shops in one trip, your hourly rate has now increased substantially. Yet if you did each of them separately with driving time and gas, it would not be worth your time. This holds true even for higher-paying shops. Do your best to do shops that are in the same area together. Also, use the directions web site on Yahoo under the "maps" link to map out the best directions so you can easily go from one location to another as quickly as possible.

Here's a thought on a way to group assignments together that makes those complex assignments more fun by giving you a much-needed mental break. Use a low-paying fast food assignment to take yourself out for breakfast or lunch in the same area while doing an apartment shop for example. So now you've gotten two shops in with minimal effort and had a meal to boot (you've got to eat anyway). Just watch your waistline—if the shop permits, mix in a salad!

3. <u>Try to Get Regular Gigs</u>

While they are rare, sometimes a particular type of shop—especially in retail—will lend itself to using the same shopper for several months. Having steady shops that you know you can count on certainly helps keep your earnings up. Plus, you may be able to take on other assignments in the same area knowing that you are going there anyway (the "grouping assignments together" strategy) to maximize your earnings.

I once did a weekly and a bi-weekly shop for the same company for two different locations of the same retail store. Each of the two was at a major mall, so not only could I count on their $100 per month, there were always shops from other companies that I could take on at these malls, so my earnings grew steadily. This would also work well for locations in your immediate neighborhood where you do your personal shopping and running of errands every day, or one you go to all the time for other reasons like a doctor's appointment or to work out. This is where taking on a lower-paying, but easy and steady "gig" will make sense.

4. Come to the Rescue of a Scheduler or Mystery Shopping Company

The more flexible your schedule, the more money you'll make. If a mystery shopping company or scheduler knows that you are a good, professional mystery shopper that they can turn to when a rush assignment or cancellation comes in, you will get these assignments offered directly to you without having to compete with other shoppers to get them.

When you get that call or e-mail, jump in immediately if you can possibly re-arrange your schedule that day—especially if it is for a company you have not worked for before. Your grateful mystery shopping company or scheduler will remember how you came to their rescue, and you'll have an "in" with them. In fact while you are in contact, they may just offer you another shop they just received and they haven't even posted anywhere yet!

5. Wait for the Cancellations, Holiday Times or Peak Periods to Increase Your Pay for the Same Assignment

In reading the job lead boards and if you get e-mail from schedulers regularly, you'll see these familiar words in the subject lines of postings and messages: "HELP!!! Lunch Shop in Anywhere, CA Due Today!" or "Shop With Bonus, Anywhere CA!", "URGENT! Anywhere, CA Shopper Needed Today!" etc. When scanning which e-mails or postings to read out of your growing list, naturally check these out first.

This is another example where being flexible in your schedule will definitely increase your earnings. It's good old supply and demand! When a job has to be completed for a client and there is trouble finding someone to complete it, the money offered to do the job goes up. Of course this happens because a shopper who was not as responsible as you had to cancel an assignment they had previously accepted; an assignment's location is not popular; or a rush job came in from a client. This is your lucky day, because with a cancellation, the company and/or scheduler have already been disappointed, so you step into a situation where by doing the right thing, you'll shine and be remembered.

So the same apartment shop you saw going for $25 is now offering a $5 bonus or more. Or maybe that car dealership shop is now worth $40. I have also seen lunch or dinner shops that were reimbursement-only deals, suddenly have a $5 or $10 bonus thrown in. By the way, the food and apartment shops, by far, seem to have the most "cries for help".

Sometimes, just because shops are scheduled during a holiday period, there will be other bonuses offered so the scheduler knows the job will get done as their usually reliable shoppers turn to other things. One Christmas, a scheduler, because she was going on vacation, offered to pay an innovative extra bonus out of her own pocket for service shops that were normally going for $20. The deal was that you would get an extra dollar added to your pay for each day you got the shop report in ahead of the due date. A bonus of up to $7 was available since the deadline was in a week. You better believe that I and the other shoppers who snatched up that assignment got our reports in 6 to 7 days early so we got paid $26 or $27 for that shop rather than $20!

While these "cries for help" can happen anytime, be especially alert at month's end, and during holidays, when the most cancellations and desperate schedulers seem to exist. It's a win-win situation. You help them out, and in return, get paid more than usual for the same assignment. In fact, I have found for certain schedulers that they almost always seem to have a crisis that I can rescue them from, so I stopped putting in for their assignments when they were first posted earlier in the month and waited for the "HELP" e-mail so that I could get better pay for the same assignment. This is easy to do once you already have done a good amount of work for the month so you can be choosier about your jobs as the month progresses. Learn the "crisis" patterns in your market and profit from them.

6. <u>Focus on The Shops That Pay The Most—Service Category Assignments & Audio/Video Mystery Shopping</u>

This might seem like a no-brainer, but you'd be surprised how many shoppers contact me with the complaint that they aren't making much money as a mystery shopper, and then when I ask them what types of assignments they are doing, they are only doing low-paying retail or fast-food shops because that's what they really like to do. It's okay to have fun as a mystery shopper, but you can be paying a high price to be a "mall rat" in lost income.

Service shops, dinner restaurant shops (in reimbursement) and purchase/return retail shops tend to pay the highest from among shops that do not involve using additional equipment, as they are the most complex and usually require a page or two of narrative. These were your apartment, homebuilder, office space, gym, car dealer, oil change, financial service shops (and anything else that falls in this category) paying at least $20 to $25 and up. You can expect most service-related shops to pay between $20 and $50 apiece. If you're really going to make money as a mystery shopper, learn to love these jobs!

On another note, service and restaurant shops are also preferable because in doing retail shops you may be tempted to spend the money you're earning, and then some at the local mall or shopping center. You're less likely to spend by doing an apartment shop or bank shop. Be careful at those car dealer shops though—you don't want to let them talk you into a new car (unless you really need one)!

For those of you who have not done many service category shops, you may want to get a copy of my other book *The Perfect Work-At-Home Job: Mystery Shopping* with its 25-page chapter nine: *Common Types of Shops: Are They Worth Your Time?* that includes details on all the high-paying service category shops, including: apartments, gyms, car dealers, oil changes, airport/travel plazas, restaurants and the rare web site and phone shops. Each shop type featured covers the following: What is it? What's involved? What to ask before you accept? The pay range for each shop. Worth Your Time?

Time Management Tips and some other bonus tips. It can be purchased 24/7 at http://www.mysteryshoppercoach.com/books.html.

By getting comfortable with technology—using digital cameras, audiotape recorders and video surveillance equipment, you can also provide a significant boost to your earnings. Shoppers who do shops that require the use of such items will often receive much higher pay or the opportunity to do big batches of assignments. They also have an edge over shoppers who do not have this technology at their disposal (when not loaned by the shopping company), or who are not open to using it in their work. Video mystery shoppers can earn from $20 to $100 per shop! See chapter twelve: *Video Mystery Shopping* for more details on this specialized aspect of mystery shopping.

7. Get in as Many Schedulers' Databases as Possible

As you have already seen, I am a bigger believer in getting known by the independent schedulers who hold the key to <u>many</u> jobs from <u>many</u> different companies, rather than an individual company that only deals with their own assignments. Although there are also some great schedulers out there who are worth knowing that just deal in their own companies' jobs.

I cannot stress enough how important it is to regularly apply to job leads from schedulers (independent and company-specific) to get in their databases for future assignments. Many schedulers work together and will share your information with their colleagues within their own company, or friends of theirs who are schedulers. Just one contact can result in a lot of exposure, so think what many contacts will do for you!

However, don't assume that just because you contacted one scheduler from Kern or Palm, for example, that you are in all of their schedulers' databases. Make contact with them all as they may specialize by type of assignments; change jobs they handle or companies they represent; new schedulers start all the time; and some like to keep their own databases. I am always amazed that just when I think I've seen every "KSS" or "PSS" e-mail address out there, another one pops up! (If you've used registered centrally with Palm or Kern, you are theoretically covered—still, if you hear from an individual scheduler from one of these two companies, I would still include in my response my information as if I might not be in their database and want to be sure).

In addition, it can't hurt to contact a scheduler for future consideration even if they are not posting a job in your particular area. For example, you see a posting for California, but it's in another part of the state. The chances are the scheduler will handle assignments for other cities in California, but just doesn't have a specific job right now. By making contact in advance, you'll be in their database or possibly referred to a colleague or friend of theirs. Keep in mind though that this should not be abused. I wouldn't contact a scheduler with a Florida job lead posting only and tell her to keep you in mind for California. You can tweak the Job Lead Response Letter in the Resource Section for this purpose.

8. Do Shops When You Travel

Between the job lead boards and the web sites of companies you work with, you are able to monitor job leads for all over the United States and Canada (and perhaps even abroad). Don't forget that you can also mystery shop when you are in another location away from home either for other work you do; when visiting family; or when traveling on vacation. This is the time to read those job lead postings from other states that you would normally ignore.

Now you probably aren't going to want to do an apartment shop when your trip purpose is to lie on the beach in Hawaii. But maybe there are a couple of lunch or dinner shops you can do so you can help stretch your travel budget and possibly eat at a better place than you might have budgeted for.

Before you travel, be sure to check out all your usual lead sources to see if there is anything doing in the city you'll be in that appeals to you. Another idea is to drop a quick e-mail to the schedulers you normally work with telling them your travel plans, and asking if they either have, or can keep you in mind, for any assignments in that area. Ask them to please pass that information along to any scheduler colleagues or friends that might handle shops for your travel destination as well.

Tip: There is a group in Delphi Forums called Reliable Traveling Shoppers located at http://forums.delphiforums.com/travelingms/start. Here you can find shops from companies open to working with

*shoppers who are traveling to their area, as well as list
your future availability in a city to which you are traveling.*

9. Be Open to Non-Shopper Jobs

As you do your mystery shopper work, you've probably
noticed other opportunities for similar flexible schedule,
independent contractor work or maybe even taken some
of this work on. From time-to-time, I see requests for
merchandisers, inventory auditors or demonstrators show
up on the mystery shopping lead boards and some
individual companies also handle this kind of work for their
clients. You almost never see the one additional job that
nearly every shopper wants—to be a <u>scheduler</u>. I
constantly get asked by shoppers "how do I become a
scheduler"? The answer is in chapter ten: *The Brass
Ring: Scheduling*, but know that it's tough since you must
network, network, network!

For the benefit of those who don't know. A <u>merchandiser</u>
is someone who goes to retail stores and may be
responsible for changing brochures in display racks;
setting up promotional displays; delivering some
materials; and liaisoning with the store manager. By the
way, combining merchandising and mystery shopping
creates a dual, home-based career that can't be beat! If
you are interested in finding out more information, check
out the new merchandising section on my web site at
<u>www.mysteryshoppercoach.com/merchandising.html</u> and
my book *The Quick And Easy Guide To Making Money As
A Merchandiser* available 24/7 from
<u>http://www.mysteryshoppercoach.com/books.html</u>.

An <u>inventory auditor</u> may be asked to do counts of merchandise or possibly re-sticker the pricing on products. Finally, a <u>demonstrator</u> is the person you see in a grocery store, or other retail location that hands out samples and coupons (note this usually involves weekend and night work).

Once you are well known and do excellent work for some of your schedulers and mystery shopping companies, you may be offered the opportunity to provide clerical assistance to a company or a scheduler. Plus, if you write well, you may be given editing assignments to tidy up the written reports of other shoppers who are not as well skilled in written communication as you are. I have received many compliments on my narratives for mystery shops and have picked up such assignments from a couple of companies myself. They are great for reliable income you can count on each month.

If you are interested in getting report editing work, you can follow my example. For me, the way I got my opportunity was that I saw a post on a job lead board and applied for it, but was too late. However, it did give me the idea that if this scheduling company needed help, maybe others did too. So whenever I got a compliment after I handed in one of my shops with a detailed narrative, I would write back, thank them and mention that in addition to my mystery shopping work, I did report editing for companies and schedulers to help them out with reports from other shoppers who were not as skilled in written communication. It worked and I got some editing assignments that way.

I also had one of my companies that I regularly shop for contact me one day and say they were putting together a group of their shoppers who would be willing to do editing and my scheduler there highly recommended me—would I be interested? So that's how it happened for me. I seized the opportunity when compliments were thrown my way, and kept turning in top work that was noticed. I would add that you could probably bring up the subject with any mystery shopping companies or schedulers that you have a very good relationship with.

Any of these "non-shopper" assignments may be something you want to pursue to round out your mystery shopping work and add to your earnings. I always say keep an open mind, make connections, be a professional and you never know what opportunities may present themselves!

10. <u>Stay in Touch With Schedulers or Companies Who You Haven't Worked With in Awhile</u>

Once you get established where you are included in many schedulers' databases; have a few regular mystery shopping companies that you work with; and monitor select job lead sources on a daily basis, you probably will have all the assignments you desire (and them some). But if you are looking for work, it never hurts to drop a quick, polite e-mail reminding a scheduler of:

- work you have done together in the past;

- the cities your shop in;

- the kinds of shops you do; and
- that since you enjoyed working with them in the past, you would be happy to have the opportunity to do so again soon.

This message is basically a version of the Shopper Job Lead Response message. Please see the Resource Section for a sample. I have used this when I have been away on vacation, so I can let everyone know I am back and available. By doing so, I have picked up some assignments to get me up and running again quickly.

Chapter Nine: Notes/Questions

Chapter Ten: The Brass Ring: Becoming A Scheduler

As I mentioned in the last chapter, becoming a scheduler seems to be every shopper's secret fantasy. In some ways, it does deserve the reputation of being a "cushy" job. Since you're not mystery shopping, you don't have to drive anywhere, create a believable scenario or write long narratives. However, if you still do want to go out in the field on shops (many schedulers do both scheduling and shopping), you can grab the plum assignment that just came in for yourself. Other major advantages are that you get to work completely at home, rather than being home-based, your schedule is totally flexible and you have the potential to make a lot more money. The experienced schedulers who were willing to share figures with me have verified that they can make up to $2,500 a month.

Okay, so what's the downside? Scheduling also can be one big headache. Your clients expect their research assignments to be booked. So you may have to work extra hours early in the morning or late at night in order to find a shopper to fill those jobs. While you can choose some of the hours you work, evening hours often come with the territory. Schedulers must be available to the clients for whom they book jobs. Plus, since many shoppers do have "day jobs", you frequently must be available in the evenings for shopper questions and to contact them for job bookings. As the scheduler, you are now on the other side of those "HELP, HELP!" and "URGENT, SHOPPER NEEDED YESTERDAY!" lead e-mails because you had an area with no takers or, more likely, a shopper let you down. Schedulers call these "flaky" shoppers (at least that's the polite term).

As a shopper, you know that you do not get paid if you fail to do the assignment correctly. Schedulers also do not get paid if you let them down for the same reasons. You also won't get paid any faster or more frequently as a scheduler than you do as a mystery shopper. Schedulers have the same problem as shoppers do with sporadic income and time lags between when they book their shops and when they get their money. A scheduler who invoices their clients for work done in February, will not see their checks until the end of March.

So you still want to be a scheduler? Okay. Well in order to do so, you generally have to prove yourself as a superb, reliable shopper first. Almost every scheduler I know was a mystery shopper with lots of experience before they went into that line of work. If you can show you're dependable and turn in high-quality work in the shopper role, your potential employer will know the type of work they can expect from you, and you'll have a better shot at a scheduling opportunity. In addition, all the networking you do as a shopper can pay off. It is often the old "who you know" that gets you the job, as the competition for scheduling is much fiercer than it is for mystery shopping assignments.

Schedulers also need to be very proficient with computers and software. If just working with Word gives you fits and you still don't know how to work with e-mailed attachments, this might not be the profession for you. In addition to the standard e-mail, word processing and spreadsheet software we use as shoppers, schedulers must be pros with database software—whether they are maintaining their own shopper databases, using their company's software or both. Plus the new automated scheduling systems represent more software that must be learned.

While work often comes in waves, as a scheduler, plan to be busiest around the beginning and end of a quarter as many projects are assigned by clients on such a basis. From a monthly standpoint, as you might expect, many projects start at the beginning of a month. That's when you will post ads, assign shops and handle a lot of correspondence. At month's end, there is lots of follow-up, rushing to meet deadlines, and, most importantly, you need to create invoices and send them out so you ultimately get your money. You may not be doing narratives, but there's still tons of paperwork.

One other thing to keep in mind is that the same automation that you may not be wild about as a shopper is also impacting the scheduling side of the business. For example, the SASSIE system used by Kern Scheduling and several mystery shopping companies is becoming popular. This innovation certainly helps a scheduler take some of the drudgery out of their work. However, it may reduce the demand for schedulers overall. Fewer schedulers could be needed due to automation, and individual mystery shopping companies that had been farming things out to independent schedulers could decide not to outsource anymore because the work has become more streamlined.

Despite the challenges, most schedulers stick with it, which is probably why it is so hard to get a scheduling job. There simply aren't enough of them for all the shoppers who want to get involved. So keep up your top-quality mystery shopping work (as if you needed an incentive anyway), so you stand out from the crowd. It will benefit you in securing more assignments and better-paying ones. And who knows, the company you work with as a shopper today, just could be the ticket to your dream scheduling job tomorrow!

Many thanks again to super scheduler Gina Olsen of Kern Scheduling for kindly sharing her insights with me in an interview previously published in my free monthly e-zine Perfect Work-At-Home Job Update (subscribe by e-mail to mscoach@aweber.com).

Chapter Ten: Notes/Questions

Chapter Eleven: Top Secret! Finding Specialized Shops And Related Opportunities—Travel, Audio/Video Shops, Focus Groups, And More!

One of the questions I frequently receive from experienced shoppers is "I've been mystery shopping for awhile but I can never seem to get a fine dining restaurant shop, a hotel shop, a travel shop (that's not a bus station), or a (insert the shop of your dreams here) shop. How do I find companies who do this?"

First, the competition for the "glamorous" travel shops is fierce. In all my time as a mystery shopper, I have only done one hotel shop myself which came through one of my regular scheduler connections.   I believe that a lot of this industry's research work is carried out by their own employees and industry insiders. Plus many hotels and travel companies provide trips for free review to travel journalists so they get feedback that way as well (is it objective though, who knows). If you're going to get involved in the travel-related shops, it would be very helpful to have experience in the field (by the way, your "past experience" of being able to successfully go on vacation doesn't count), so that you stand out from the typical mystery shoppers applying.

I know though that many of you have your hearts set on getting a shop in these and other areas that may hold a particular interest for you, so here's how you track these companies down. And because you are looking to do a shop that is hard to obtain, and you are an experienced shopper, this is one of the times that I feel it is fine to sign up directly with companies. Just realize that actually getting an assignment in your desired specialized shop category it is a bit of a long shot, but as you have some time, feel free to apply to those companies that serve that particular industry.

Go to www.mysteryshop.org. That's the Mystery Shoppers Providers Association (MSPA) web site. It's the trade organization for companies that provide mystery shopping services. It's not an organization for shoppers, although they do offer some tools for shoppers—like the Shopper Bulletin Board (not very effective as mostly I have found it to be people listing their availability--like some busy scheduler has nothing better to do than scroll through hundreds of unorganized posts--and newbies asking "how do I get started?")

On the front page, choose "North America" (unless you want a country outside the United States, and then "Members". At the top of that page, it says "Search MSPA Companies" (ignore the warning that says "if you are a shopper seeking mystery shopping companies, please do not use this page ☺), and clicking that link takes you to a page where there is currently a green button that says "Search MSPA Member Companies" with the sentence "Click on the green button to look for MSPA member companies to develop and manage your mystery shopping program" below it.

Now you've hit the mother lode, **but please see the VERY IMPORTANT NOTE BELOW!** Here you can select your geographic region, the industry you are looking for (i.e. lodging) and the category or type of shops within that industry if you so desire (i.e. Mystery Shopping or focus groups) to further refine your inquiry. Then just click "submit", and you'll get a neat list of every company that meets your criteria. Now not *every* mystery shopping company in the world is going to be listed as the site is just for MSPA members. But all the top companies are members, so if one is not a member they could be a pretty small player.

Now that you know about this tool, think of the other possibilities. Suppose you want to find companies in your area that now offer the hot video mystery shopping field I will introduce you to in the next chapter *Video Mystery Shopping?* Just select "video recorded mystery shopping" in the "by category" drop-down menu. Want to find audio-recorded shops? Select it under the category menu. They even have merchandising, focus group and inventory audits for those of you who enjoy that kind of work. Have some fun "playing" with the category search function and see what the possibilities are in your area! Use a tweaked version of letter #6—"Touching Base" in the Resource Section of this book if you mail or e-mail companies who don't have a web site where you can apply—**but please see the important note that follows next before doing so.**

As you may have noticed upon accessing it, the MSPA does not really want shoppers using this tool, since this information is for potential business clients for the member companies. So, if you apply to a company you have researched in this fashion via their web site or, if they don't have a web site and you want to call, e-mail or write to them, just don't mention that you got the contact information from the MSPA web site. If too many shoppers end up bothering the companies based on the information being on the site as a source, they might pull it or password-protect it and then we'll lose the chance to use this technique. So mum's the word!

Chapter Eleven: Notes/Questions

Chapter Twelve: Video Mystery Shopping: The New Frontier

One of the hottest and most controversial trends to hit the mystery shopping profession is what is known as "video mystery shopping". Like it's ancestor, audio mystery shopping, shoppers who perform this type of work, must use very small equipment (this is not the camera that you have been using to take pictures of your kids or on your latest vacation), that they hide within their clothing or other appropriate items. The purpose is to capture the actual interaction with the client's employee(s) as well as to show how the overall location, or specific portions like a customer service desk or cash register check-out, looked at that particular date and time. Video recording can catch things like mismatched sales presentations where a salesperson says one thing, but his or her body language says another.

The big advantages of video mystery shopping are:

- <u>the shops are much higher-paying than the non-technology-based mystery shop</u>.

Video mystery shoppers can earn anywhere from $20 to $100 a shop. So many veteran mystery shoppers are jumping on the bandwagon and are often doubling the income they make. It's now very possible for an experienced, professional mystery shopper who lives in or near a major market area to make as much as $2,000 in one month's time. As these shops gain in popularity and more mystery shopping companies make them available to their clients, those figures could increase (of course the competition among shoppers for the work will likely also be on the rise).

- <u>you don't have to provide a report after the shop</u>.

That's right, no more narratives, and no long list of questions because your report was neatly captured on video tape. So in effect, your hourly wage can go up substantially with video mystery shopping, because the total time you need to devote to the shop decreases because of the lack of a written report. This is also a plus for those of you who are not gifted writers and struggle over narratives. At the end of the shop you simply mail in your report (postage is reimbursed), and you're done.

- <u>the proof is in the tape</u>

Since your whole shop is captured on video, there is no room for dispute over whether or not the shop was performed correctly.

Sounds too good to be true? Here's the flip side:

- <u>you're much more accountable</u>

With the entire shop video-recorded, if you, as the shopper, do not follow the shop guidelines, it will be very obvious—there is no room to fudge anything (not that you ever would).

- <u>you have to be very comfortable using technology</u>

Since the video tape is your only record of the shop and serves as your report, if something goes awry, you can't stop the shop and say "technical difficulties, please stand by". If the battery goes mid-shop, or the focus is off, you will be asked to do the shop over without additional compensation, or the mystery shopping company may simply choose not to pay you at all.

- <u>you must be able to still conduct your shop in as natural a fashion as if the shop was being done without equipment</u>.

Some shoppers get nervous enough just doing a regular assignment, feeling as if a big label "Mystery Shopper" is on their forehead. You may feel even more jittery knowing you are walking around concealing a camera and knowing that your work is being taped. (You can overcome this both with experience and getting used to the equipment on your own before you do the job).

- <u>making an investment in the video equipment used to do this work could be required</u>

Some companies provide it and maintain it, some do not. I would advise you to only work with companies that do let you use their equipment and perform the necessary maintenance, until you have some experience in this area and know that it is something you want to do for the long-term.

Such a purchase may be tax-deductible as a business expense, please check with your tax advisor.

- this aspect of mystery shopping is starting to step on the toes of private investigator work, as you are now, in effect, doing video surveillance.

Therefore, the laws in your city, county or state may be different once you start doing video or even audio shops as opposed to those for which you do not use technology. You may now be required to have a private investigator license where you did not previously need one. Look into this for yourself. Do not rely on any mystery shopping company or scheduler to know the correct information for your state. As an independent contractor, you are responsible for knowing the laws and complying with them. The same web site I mentioned earlier in Chapter Three: *Are You Legal?* will help you look up the private investigator laws applicable to your state (if any). It is located at www.crimetime.com/licensing.htm.

One of my *Perfect Work-At-Home Job Update* monthly e-zine subscribers (subscribe for free by e-mail to mscoach@aweber.com), Margie, from Washington state, was kind enough to provide the basis for some of the information above, and recently shared with me her feelings about video mystery shopping based on her experiences (she is also a frequent audio tape mystery shopper).

First, for those of you who are concerned about the ethics of employee video taping, you shouldn't be. Most employers now have items in the paperwork employees sign when they come on board (especially in retailing and other industries where there is heavy interaction with the public) that notify them and/or cover the company with regard to audio, video and e-mail monitoring.

Some companies just come right out and tell their employees that they use video mystery shopping programs, so they know it's kind of like the old Candid Camera television program—you never know when someone will say "smile, you're on Candid Camera" (I guess that program may have been the first video mystery shopping effort). Except it's not usually that immediate— the employee doesn't find out exactly when they were taped until later on. As Margie explained to me: "The employees that I shop are well aware that they will be audio or video recorded by a mystery shopper. The employee then watches their own tape as a part of their training or performance evaluation (however the client chooses to use it)."

Margie had a really plum assignment recently for one of the companies she works with as a video mystery shopper. It seems that she was asked to go along on a new home shop to pose as the wife of another male shopper. For her time, she got paid $35 and she did not even carry the equipment! As Margie puts it "No report, no paperwork, just $35 for going along for the ride! Well, you do need to send in a quick summary of any follow-up you receive, but it is only a short paragraph. You can't really beat that for easy work, and it's a lot more fun with a partner, you can really get into your acting skills as you try to play off of one another." (No don't expect all of your video mystery shopping assignments to be this easy, but I think you get the idea of what is possible).

I have recently received a lot of inquiries about this type of work from the shoppers who read my free monthly e-zine *Perfect Work-At-Home Job Update* (subscribe by e-mail to mscoach@aweber.com), and visit my web site Mystery Shopper Coach's Corner at http://www.mysteryshoppercoach.com. Most are interested, but are reluctant to move forward on this opportunity. They have mentioned that they feel very uncomfortable with the idea of taping their shops and targets.

To me, whether this is a fad or actually becomes a regular and widely-available form of mystery shopping, remains to be seen. The initial concept and feedback I have received from those who are doing this work is very encouraging and this specialization could represent a real boost to mystery shopper income. So I advise you to keep an open mind and watch for assignments that do not require you to purchase or lease equipment through your usual channels. Also feel free to use the MSPA tool I showed you in the last chapter to apply directly to some companies as you have some time. You do not need to pay anyone to register to be a video mystery shopper or to participate in any kind of a paid directory or listing.

Please note: I would love to hear from those of you who are doing this work and let me know what you think— positive or negative. You just might get featured in an upcoming edition of *Perfect Work-At-Home Job Update* e-zine or in a revised edition of this book!

Chapter Twelve: Notes/Questions

Chapter Thirteen: Power Negotiating For Higher Shop Fees

Obviously, in your mystery shopping work, you want to make the most money per shop. So you focus on the service category and technology-based shops where possible, take the higher-paying purchase and return retail shops and if you accept a low-paying shop, you do so in combination with other such shops or merchandising assignments for an overall improved hourly rate. You even use (or at least will start using) my tip of trying for mileage reimbursement when an urgent shop is far away. But here's something you may not know—your shop fees may be negotiable!

That's right. If you think just because a job says it pays "X", that this is only what the fee can be, you could be mistaken at times and letting mystery shopping income slip through your fingers. Think about it, the mystery shopping company wants to pay an amount that will entice you to do the job, yet still be as little as possible so they keep more of their client's fee. A scheduler does not want to have to bonus an assignment unless they are desperate to book the gig because it may very well come out of their end. Plus, the company or scheduler is figuring that your report will need editing work, where that may not be the case and that's another expense to them.

So how do you get either a mystery shopping company or scheduler to up the ante? If you are a proven, very experienced shopper, particularly in the service categories where you are a veteran of top-notch narratives, you are worth a great deal to mystery shopping companies, schedulers and their clients. You offer superior quality in your work, your reports barely need to be edited (if at all) and you can be counted on to get the shop done on time with your report submitted before the deadline. It is because of this, you may very well be able to negotiate a higher fee for taking on an assignment from time-to-time. In the "real world", a more highly-qualified candidate makes a higher hourly wage or salary. Why should it always be that all mystery shoppers receive the same shop fee regardless of their qualifications?

Your best chance of negotiating a higher shop fee will be under one or more of the following circumstances:

- it's a complicated, narrative-intensive shop;

- it's a shop category in which you are an expert;

- it's a rush shop;

- you were contacted by the company or scheduler for the shop directly

- before it was posted all over;

- this is a company or scheduler with whom you have a strong relationship who knows the caliber of your work and ability to meet deadlines; and

- it's a shop that is posted all over that is still available with the deadline approaching.

Of course, if this is a highly popular shop with lots of takers, it's not the time to try this—you'll have enough trouble just getting the gig. But if the shop meets one or more of the above criteria, here's how to try for a few more bucks.

Picture this scenario. You get a call or e-mail from one of your favorite schedulers and there is an apartment shop that is overdue because of a prior shopper cancellation. It's a targeted shop with two pages of narrative and it's due in two days. The pay is either not mentioned, or it is indicated as an amount that is the same as they always pay.

Start off by telling the scheduler how much you appreciate her/him thinking of you for this assignment and you would love to help. <u>However… and pause for just a moment</u> (this "however and pause" is very important because the scheduler was breathing a sigh of relief that you were going to save the day for them and now you don't sound so sure). Then ask "what are you paying"? Or if you were already told the shop pays the same as always, say politely "isn't $XX what you always pay for this assignment"? By the way, I regularly see a couple of schedulers that are well-known who keep asking for help in their e-mail leads and postings over and over, yet they keep quoting the same pay. Is it any wonder why their jobs are not getting taken? You can use this to your advantage.

The first question "what are you paying" may automatically make the scheduler feel like you aren't going to be satisfied with the typical amount, and they

may just come right out and say, "well I can go $X"
(should be at least $5 more than is standard). If they say
that the pay is the same as they always offer for this job,
go on to the step discussed next.

In the case where the amount was already specified, the
scheduler may verify the same fee and add that they are
unable to offer a bonus. In that case, you can politely say
something along the lines of: "I would love to help you out,
and you know based on our work together that it will be a
quality report done on time. Since it's a rush job with a lot
of narrative, are you sure you could not offer even a $5
bonus?" A politely-phrased question like this reminds the
scheduler that you are one of their best shoppers, they
can count on you and that this is a special request on their
part that deserves something above the standard fee. It
will be a great test to see if there is really any flexibility in
the fee or not.

This will either get you more money (congratulations), or
the scheduler will still insist that she/he is sorry, but they
can't go any higher and ask again if you want the job. If
you can't get more money, you can decide for yourself if
you still want to do the assignment or not based on your
own personal situation (like you could use the money that
month). By the way, if you are short money and can use
the gig, never let that be known upfront—you will not have
any negotiating power because they know you will take
the job.

Suppose the situation is instead one where you see the
same job posted or e-mailed to you over and over with
increasingly urgent "please help" headings? You can use

the same ideas above to respond to the lead. Particularly if it is a company you have not dealt with before, provide your usual professional response (see the Resource Section for examples), but emphasize that you are able to help with this shop that is obviously very urgent to them. Plus, make sure they understand you are highly experienced, an expert in this shop category and that you will be able to do a quality job for them and get the report in on time without any problem. Then add that you did not notice a bonus being offered for this assignment, but since it is a rush job and you are highly qualified (also let them know if you are going outside of your normal shopping coverage area), you would like to know if they could possibly add a small bonus to the pay for the assignment?

Close your e-mail by repeating that you are ready to go to work for them on the job as soon as you hear from them. Then be sure to give your full contact block or signature (e-mail and phone number). Although many companies deal by e-mail exclusively, in a rush they will often pick up the phone. When you hear from them, either accept or decline the assignment based on their response and your personal financial needs.

Here's another situation where you may be able to negotiate your fee higher. If you regularly do shops that are heavy on the narrative for the same mystery shopping company and you receive compliments on your reports, see if you can politely negotiate $5 per shop more in pay on an on-going basis. You can justify this to the company by the fact that in addition to your overall professionalism, your work requires little, if any editing, so the company is saving that expense on each of your reports that is already being factored into their overall profit for that assignment. You are also saving them all-important time that would have been spent if your report needed editing. Plus, if they would have had to assign this job out to a scheduler, it would have cost them money too. Surely your work is worth another $5 per shop. I have personally been very successful in this regard. Try it!

In my former corporate life I was considered a very strong negotiator—both when I entered salary negotiations and when I negotiated contracts on behalf of my employer. The ideas I have introduced here are simply putting those concepts to work in the "mystery shopping world". I believe that power negotiating means that you achieve the "win-win" situation you often hear about. You got what you wanted, the other party got what they wanted, so you both win.

Power negotiating does not mean being nasty—you want to be polite and keep a good relationship with this person for the future. No one can blame you for politely trying to get what is fair for yourself (in fact, you will often get treated with more respect). You want to display confidence in yourself and the quality of the services you offer, but not be obnoxious. If after making one or two attempts as described above, you don't get any further, don't push it. Back off and either decline the assignment or accept it.

If you don't get additional money and still accept the job, be sure to let the scheduler know that you "understand that they can't offer you a bonus this time, but would appreciate their keeping your assistance at this urgent time in mind and either personally offer you an assignment that they receive before it gets posted around at their next opportunity, or to be sure to offer you a bonus next time when they have more flexibility in the pay". While you can say this in your own way, this is a very important point. If you accept a job after unsuccessfully getting more money without this kind of comment, you have hurt your chances for negotiating in the future under the same situation. By politely making the scheduler aware that you are giving in, but that you expect them to do something for you when it is in their power to do so in the future, you have maintained your negotiating strength. The odds are very high that this conversation will result in an extra assignment being offered directly to you, or a bonus given the next time around (if you deliver on the job you just accepted of course).

Please also note, I have complete respect for schedulers. As you know, I am a big believer that they hold the key to maximum earnings as a mystery shopper. What is the peace of mind worth to a busy scheduler who also wants to look good and meet deadlines for their client mystery shopping company? The same is true for a mystery shopping company that wants to look good for their own customer. Realize that your work and experience have value, and it can't hurt to try and get more money for yourself for a quality job (especially one done under rushed circumstances). I tried to negotiate whenever it was reasonable to do so—and I won about 75% of the time!

Remember that you will not always win in your negotiations, but if you don't ask, you'll never know if you could have gotten more pay. If you could negotiate the pay for just five assignments a month higher by $5, that's $25, or <u>the equivalent of one extra shop you did not have to actually perform that month</u>. Do that every month and <u>there is an extra $300 in your pocket over the course of the year, without any extra time spent doing shops</u>!

Chapter Thirteen: Notes/Questions

Chapter Fourteen: Now That You Know How To Finally Make Money As A Shopper, Get Going!

To put it all together, here's a summary of 9 things you need to do to increase your mystery shopper earnings:

1. Spiff Up Your "Home Office" (no more kitchen table)

Set up or improve your home office space. Change or add a new, more professional e-mail address if necessary. Create your professional voicemail message and teach others in your household how to take a proper message for you. Get hold of any software you may be missing—even freebies like Acrobat Reader® (www.adobe.com) and WinZip® (www.winzip.com).

2. Review the Resource Section

Create your own sample e-mail messages or responses to job application questions for each type you'll need:

- Sample Response To Job Lead Posting

- "Keep Me in Mind" Response (for when you don't get the job)

- "Assignment Acknowledgement" (for when you do get the job)

- "Thank You for the Assignment" (for your scheduler after you have completed the job)

- Report Submission Message (for your mystery shopping company contact)

- Touching Base (when you want to remind schedulers or mystery shopping companies you work with of your availability)

3. <u>Start Visiting the Suggested Job Lead Sources</u>

I suggest visiting the job lead resources frequently until you have identified the two or three best suited for you and you also feel you have made contact with all the schedulers who regularly serve your area. Then you can just keep tabs on them to make sure you don't miss someone new. The more jobs (again, note I said jobs, not web sites) you apply for initially, the more jobs you'll land and the more scheduler contacts you'll make *so the jobs will eventually find you!* Don't forget that you need to respond to job lead postings right away to have the best chance of landing the assignment.

Check your e-mail every two or three hours ideally including evenings, or if you have access via your cell phone or PDA, you'll always be in the know. All those extra scheduler e-mails now represent chances to earn money or eat at your favorite restaurant for free! You should see a sizable improvement in your volume, pay and scheduler job lead e-mails sent to you on a regular basis within the next 30-60 days of a consistent effort where you immediately respond to leads using all the techniques I mentioned—probably a lot sooner.

4. Set Up Or Improve Your Records

If you're guilty of not being organized, take a few steps back and drop everything till you do. Get organized and stay organized! Set up your company folders. Keep track of scheduler contacts made; companies you have signed up with (including passwords or shopper ID information); your shop assignments; and payments due. Again, please e-mail me at Melanie@mysteryshoppercoach.com for my free, cool Excel spreadsheets that will help you get organized and save you time.

5. Determine Your Mystery Shopper Earnings Goals And Create Your Plan For Reaching Them

If you have a definite number in mind for how much you want to earn each month, it's a lot easier than just saying I want to make "$X". Of course, make sure your goal is realistic given your time, your market, etc. Knowing you are now going to focus on higher-paying shops (service category and technology-based) and put all the tips in this book to use, figure out the number of shops you need and go for it!

While it may take a little while to hit your goal, you should see improvement in the number of opportunities you hear about fairly quickly. Keep in mind that despite your best efforts, mystery shopper income fluctuates based on client needs and factors such as a restriction from doing a particular shop location for a set period of time.

6. <u>Eliminate Mystery Shopper Income Drainers And Mistakes That Can Be Costing You Future Jobs And Money</u>!

Review the 9 mystery shopper income drainers and plug up those leaks right away! Making top money means doing the best things right, and eliminating the things that you are doing wrong. Plus, watch your reporting and keep everything organized post-shop so you don't miss out on the pay you've already worked to earn. Don't forget that report submission is an excellent opportunity to stand out and further market yourself in a subtle way that hardly anyone thinks of doing—don't waste it!

7. <u>Make A Commitment To Work With Schedulers And Adopt The Ways To Maximize Your Income</u>

In real estate, they say it's "location, location, location". In mystery shopping, it's "schedulers, schedulers, schedulers". If you work with some already, work with more of them and seize every opportunity to stand out. If you don't currently work with schedulers (independent and company-specific), you're going to see great things happen to your earnings when you do. Also include as many of the different tips and ways to maximize income that I have shown you throughout this book as possible. Add something new every day that you can until you are consistently hitting your income goals.

8. <u>Use "Power Negotiating" to earn higher shop fees</u>

Where appropriate, in a polite manner, try to negotiate a higher shop fee for a rush assignment for which you are contacted directly, a shop that has no takers and the company or scheduler is getting increasingly desperate, or for a company for whom you regularly do work that requires little or no editing. The little extras you negotiate for yourself could be worth hundreds of dollars a year to you!

9. Sign up for my free e-zine "*Perfect Work-At-Home Job Update*"

E-mail me at mscoach@aweber.com.   In my newsletter I answer select questions from my readers, and share some of my latest tips and news from the trenches—*the inside scoop that you've been looking for, but no one tells you.*

Also be sure to regularly check out my web site Mystery Shopper Coach's Corner at http://www.mysteryshoppercoach.com for back issues of my e-zine, tips, resources, special offers and more!

Chapter Fourteen: Notes/Questions

Chapter Fifteen: Final Thoughts

So there you have it—everything you need to finally make money as a mystery shopper. If you make the extra effort in new ways, before you know it, you'll be just like I was—with more jobs and related income opportunities coming your way than you can handle. Just don't forget that the whole purpose of doing this kind of flexible work is to use it to give yourself the life you desire. Use this flexibility to take time for yourself, your friends and loved ones, and to do the things you always say you would do "if you had more time".

Good luck with getting to the next level of your mystery shopping career! If you would like to share with me your success stories about how you have improved your income using the ideas in this book, or how the flexibility of mystery shopping has improved your life, I'd love to hear from you! E-mail me at Melanie@mysteryshoppercoach.com anytime.

Last, but not least, to really maximize your income, create a dual, flexible, home-based career by adding merchandising work to your mystery shopping. It's easy to do with my book *The Quick And Easy Guide To Making Money As A Merchandiser*. More information about merchandising and FAQs can be found at my web site Mystery Shopper Coach's Corner at www.mysteryshoppercoach.com/merchandising.html and the book is available 24/7 at http://www.mysteryshoppercoach.com/books.html.

—Melanie R. Jordan

P.S. As a special thank you for purchasing this book, I want to be sure you are kept up-to-date on any changes that many occur to some of the resources listed. Please check this special URL for any updates from time-to-time provided FREE to you!
http://www.mysteryshoppercoach.com/updates.html

P.P.S. I am constantly writing and publishing new books and special reports on a variety of topics. Please check my publishing company's web site at
http://www.sunloverpublishing.com for other publications you might enjoy!

Resource Section

<u>I. Sample E-Mail Correspondence</u>

<u>1. Sample Response To Job Lead Posting</u>

Re: Anywhere, CA Apartment Shop

Jane—

I saw your message on the Mystery Shoppers Resource web site and am available to help you with the Anywhere, CA apartment shop due June 7th. If this shop is no longer available, I would greatly appreciate your adding me to your database for future assignments.

Currently, I am regularly working with eight companies on a regular basis—Joey's Mystery Shopping, ABC Shopping, XYZ Shoppers, 123 Service, Joey's Spies, Service/Service, The Jane Doe Group and Made-Up Mystery Shopping (apartment, restaurant, retail, automotive, fitness center and other service-type shops). I am self-employed as a writer and editor with flexible hours weekdays.

With 15+ years experience in marketing and an extensive background in market research, customer service and sales training, I am a valuable asset to any research firm. I have also worked in the financial services industry and in retailing. I am observant, detail-oriented, dependable, have excellent communication skills and am PC literate.

I especially focus on shops in these cities: Anywhere, Anyplace Forest, Anytime, Nowhere Ranch, Sometime, Shopper Viejo, Mystery Beach, Service Mesa, Somewhere and Secret Point

Thank you for your time and consideration. I look forward to being of service!

Melanie Jordan
Melanie@mysteryshoppercoach.com

2. "Keep Me In Mind" Response (For When You Don't Get The Job)

Re: Your Last Message

Jane—

Thank you for getting back to me about the Anywhere, CA apartment shop. I am sorry to hear that the assignment was already filled. However, please be sure to let me know if you have a cancellation—with my flexible schedule I can usually jump right in on an assignment that another shopper was unable to deliver.

I would also greatly appreciate your adding me to your database of shoppers and keeping me in mind for future assignments. Again, I am a reliable and experienced shopper focusing on assignments in Anywhere, Anyplace Forest, Anytime, Nowhere Ranch, Sometime, Shopper Viejo, Mystery Beach, Service Mesa, Somewhere and Secret Point, CA.

Thank you for your time and consideration. I look forward to working with you soon.

Melanie Jordan
Melanie@mysteryshoppercoach.com

3. "Assignment Acknowledgement" (For When You Do Get The Job)

Re: Anywhere, CA Apartment Shop Confirmation

Jane—

Thank you for the apartment shop assignment in Anywhere, CA due June 7th at a pay rate of $25. You can count on me to meet your deadline, and I appreciate the opportunity to work with you and Joey's Mystery Shopping.

Melanie Jordan
Melanie@mysteryshoppercoach.com

Note: if this is a scheduler or company you work with fairly regularly, you can make your phrasing a little more personal like "it's always a pleasure to work with you and Joey's Mystery Shopping". Or "nice to be working with you and Joey's Mystery Shopping again".

4. "Thank You For The Assignment" After You Have Completed The Job (To Your Scheduler)

Re: Anywhere, CA Apartment Shop Completed

Jane—

I just wanted to let you know this shop was completed today and I just sent the report to Mary Jones at Joey's Mystery Shopping.

Thank you for the opportunity, and I look forward to working with you again soon. Please keep me in your database for future assignments. I focus on assignments in Anywhere, Anyplace Forest, Anytime, Nowhere Ranch, Sometime, Shopper Viejo, Mystery Beach, Service Mesa, Somewhere and Secret Point, CA.

Melanie Jordan
Melanie@mysteryshoppercoach.com

5. <u>Report Submission Message (To The Actual Mystery Shopping Company Contact</u>)

Re: Anywhere, CA—Jones Shop Completed

Mary—

Attached are two documents—one contains the Excel forms Jane Doe provided me with for this shop; the other is a separate word document with the shop narrative. Please let me know if you have any questions or difficulty with the attachments.

I greatly appreciated the opportunity to be of service for this assignment and I look forward to working with you again soon.

Melanie Jordan
<u>Melanie@mysteryshoppercoach.com</u>

<u>Note</u>: *if this is a company you work with fairly regularly, you can make your phrasing a little more personal like "it's always a pleasure to work with you". Or "nice to be working with you again".*

6. Touching Base (Looking For Work)

Re: Touching Base (or Checking In)

Hi Jane—

I recently did some apartment shops for you in Anywhere, Somewhere and Secret Point, CA. Since I have some extra time in my schedule over the next few days and enjoyed working with you, I was wondering if there were any assignments that I could help you with?

Again, I am a reliable and experienced shopper focusing on assignments in Anywhere, Anyplace Forest, Anytime, Nowhere Ranch, Sometime, Shopper Viejo, Mystery Beach, Service Mesa, Somewhere and Secret Point, CA.

Thank you for your time and consideration. I look forward to working with you again soon.

Melanie Jordan
Melanie@mysteryshoppercoach.com

II. Sample On-Site Narrative For Shopper Report

Anywhere, CA Apartment Shop
On-Site Presentation
Jane Doe
5/2/00
Shopper: Melanie Jordan

When I walked in, I was immediately greeted by a female employee who cheerfully asked if she could help me (yes, appointment with Jane). She pointed out Jane who was just finishing up with someone. The employee introduced herself as Mary—she invited me to sit at an adjoining desk and offered me refreshments. Shortly afterwards, Jane walked over, smiled, extended her hand, introduced herself and welcomed me by name.

Jane did a good job of showing the property amenities. For example, when pointing out the resort-style pool, she mentioned how it was heated all year but they turned the temperature down if it got hot in the summer. I also saw the main spa, fitness center (where she greeted another resident working out) and the laundry room ("good for washing your blankets"). We made small talk as we walked over to the model that reinforced the positives of the property like the quiet.

At the model, Jane walked me through and pointed out the features and benefits—loads of closet space, unusual angled patio that was private, white washed cabinets, cozy living room, mirrored closets in bedrooms, room sizes (showed how the smaller one was a very nice size for my home office) and how modern everything was.

She asked me how I liked it and I told her I thought it would work very nicely depending on where the actual unit was. I also asked Jane if there were any specials that she could offer because while the unit was nice, it was at the upper end of my price range. She addressed this by saying that the unit actually was on special ($1,380 vs. $1,475) and I would get $300 off move-in with a 6-month lease and $600 off with a 9-month lease.

Jane then asked me to walk with her to see the vacant apartment that was ready now on the second floor so I could see one that was not a model (we did). She next invited me to see the actual unit location of #133 that was occupied, but we walked around the back and up the stairs. My concern about this was the terrace was dark so the exposure was not sunny (she addressed this by telling me the sun would make it too hot in the summer anyway). I told Jane that everything else was right so maybe I could compromise on the terrace.

Back at the office, Jane asked me to fill out an application and leave a $100 deposit to take the unit off the market. I explained I still had two more appointments that day that I wanted to keep. Jane stressed that I wasn't going to find another 2 bedroom like this for $1,380 and the deposit was refundable within 72 hours so I could look and then change my mind. I declined but said I would be deciding in the next day or so. Jane then said to let her know as soon as possible because she "couldn't say that unit would still be there". I assured her I would, and she stood, smiled, extended her hand and thanked me for coming in.

Overall, I thought Jane did a good job with the tour of the property and the apartment. Jane listened carefully to my needs, did her best to counter my objections and tried to close me multiple times. Had I really been looking for an apartment, I would have leased from her.

III. Ordering Additional Copies of How To Finally Make Money As A Mystery Shopper

Melanie's follow-up book is *How-To Finally Make Money As A Mystery Shopper*. This 140-page resource is designed to help the experienced shopper who just isn't making the money they desire get to that next level of mystery shopper earnings.

It takes the best of the material from *The Perfect Work-At-Home Job: Mystery Shopping* and adds chapters, tips and resources you won't want to miss! Plus, the content-packed chapters called *Power Negotiating For Higher Mystery Shopper Fees* and a section on *Getting What's Coming To You*, along with ones on scheduling, video mystery shopping and finding specialized shops that alone are worth the price of the book.

Please note that there is some overlap of material between the two books, but there is lots of unique content in each. Check out the table of contents on-line at the URLs listed below to see if this book is for you. You can also order one for your experienced shopper friends and family—it's a great gift idea! It may be purchased 24/7 as follows.

For a pdf file viewable by PC or Mac using Adobe Acrobat's reader (available as a free download from www.adobe.com if you don't have it), go to:

http://www.booklocker.com/books/924.html

Please cut and paste the URL into your browser and then hit enter.

Please note that all of these e-book files go through a complete virus scan before they are made available for download on Booklocker.com (my book sales site host). You can count on the file you download to be clean and safe!

To make an e-book purchase using PayPal™ funds, a check or money order, please e-mail me at Melanie@mysteryshoppercoach.com for instructions on making your purchase directly through me.

What others are saying about this book:

"I loved your book! Thanks for all the great leads and hints. I have used all your ideas and techniques and so far have received 11 new assignments in the last 18 days!"--Lara O., Arlington Heights, IL

"I used one of your tips about getting more money for shops at the end of the month and I received $35 and $32 for two shops that normally pay $25 apiece! This is the best part-time job I have ever had."--Vicky M., Seattle, WA

"You have put together a well-written, wonderful resource that is a pleasure to read and is offering me so much information that I just didn't have before."--J. Knight, Boston, MA

IV. About The Quick And Easy Guide To Making Money As A Merchandiser

Order additional copies of *The Quick And Easy Guide To Making Money As A Merchandiser* for your friends, family and even your fellow mystery shoppers—it's a great gift idea! It may be purchased 24/7 as follows:

For a pdf file viewable by PC or Mac using Adobe Acrobat's reader (available as a free download from www.adobe.com if you don't have it), go to:

http://www.booklocker.com/books/948.html

Please cut and paste the URL into your browser and then hit enter.

Please note that all of these e-book files go through a complete virus scan before they are made available for download on Booklocker.com (my book sales site host). You can count on the file you download to be clean and safe.

Or for a print copy of this book, it's also available from Booklocker.com at:

http://www.booklocker.com/books/948.html

To purchase this e-book using PayPal™ funds, a check or money order, please e-mail me at Melanie@mysteryshoppercoach.com for instructions on making your purchase directly through me.

Here's what others are saying about this book:

"I purchased your book "The Quick And Easy Guide To Making Money As A Merchandiser" a few days ago and just today I received my first assignment. And it's a year-round situation doing resets/revisions in a local store. I truly appreciate your book!"--Chell S., Tyler, TX

"I ordered your book on Saturday, read the whole thing and started using the information the next day. On Wednesday I got my first assignment for a major discount retailer! On Friday I got another job to do at two other stores near my home. I can't believe how quickly I got leads in my area. Thank you for the great book and great new career!"--Natalie B., Weston, WI

"Your book is packed with great ideas and suggestions--I couldn't put it down! I found the merchandising field was a pretty closely guarded secret, for which it was very hard to get any information. That is why I like and appreciate your book so much!"--Helen P., Jacksonville, FL

V. About The Perfect Work-At-Home Job: Mystery Shopping

Melanie's classic 161-page book *The Perfect Work-At-Home Job: Mystery Shopping* is a great resource for the newbie or beginning shopper, as well as those who might never have otherwise thought about the possibility of mystery shopping as a work-at-home career. It's a great gift idea! It may be purchased 24/7 as follows:

For a pdf file viewable by PC or Mac using Adobe Acrobat's reader (available as a free download from www.adobe.com if you don't have it), go to:

http://www.booklocker.com/books/923.html

Please cut and paste the URL into your browser and then hit enter.

Please note that all of these e-book files go through a complete virus scan before they are made available for download on Booklocker.com (my book sales site host). You can count on the file you download to be clean and safe.

To make an e-book purchase using PayPal™ funds, a check or money order, please e-mail me at Melanie@mysteryshoppercoach.com for instructions on making your purchase directly through me.

Here's what others are saying about this book:

"I bought both of your mystery shopping books 3 weeks ago and they've helped me get off to a great start. I booked 11 shops for $290 in shop fees and $162 in restaurant reimbursements for a total of $452!"--C. Wilson, Los Angeles, CA

"The day I bought your book changed my life! I have followed your advice, almost to the letter, and it has paid off in spades. In the last three weeks I have done over 35 mystery shops and I am currently scheduled to perform approximately fifteen more over the next week. Many of the shops I have completed included bonuses for upcoming deadlines or remote areas."-- Patrick B., Richmond, VA

"Thanks again for providing a great book for those who want to become mystery shoppers. Friday night I started following your tips and visiting the suggested websites. I was offered my first mystery shopping job on Monday morning! Since then, I have accepted two more and actually completed my first job!"--M.S., Louisville, KY

"I think the resources you provide to mystery shoppers are incredibly valuable. I put your advice into practice and accepted my first apartment shop. I had a blast and have completed 8 more apartment shops and a fitness shop. I spent under $30 for both books and the apartment shops more than made up for it at $20-$30 apiece!"--H. Lewis, Vancouver, WA

"I just purchased both of your mystery shopping books and am pleased to say that I already got a transportation shop and two retail shops. Thank you for all of the advice on how to get started the right way. You stress the importance of being both professional and organized, and I cannot agree with you more.--Ann-Marie M., Atlanta, GA

VI. About Secret Mystery Shopping Sites Revealed!

Available by special order only at Melanie's web site Mystery Shopper Coach's Corner at http://www.mysteryshoppercoach.com/secretsites.html.

How would you like to actually know that you have a mystery shopping assignment when you see one announced, rather than wait to have it assigned to you? How about the ability to work more efficiently by grouping assignments together? Or even a way to hear about mystery shopping assignments in even the smallest cities and towns?

There's a new way to get some of your mystery shopping assignments, and when you combine it with the sure-fire techniques I discuss in *The Perfect Work-At-Home Job: Mystery Shopping* and *How-To Finally Make Money As A Mystery Shopper*, you'll be able to take control of your mystery shopper income and career like never before! Get your copy of *Secret Mystery Shopping Sites Revealed!* today at http://www.mysteryshoppercoach.com/secretsites.html.

What others are saying about this book:
"Great shopping tips! I devoured your book "Secret Mystery Shopping Sites Revealed!" I guess I was off to a good start, but I was able to get some very helpful info, new leads and tips."—D. Krohn, Bristol, RI

"Thank you for your precious and valuable insights!"-- Trevis B., Brooklyn, NY

VII. Ever Thought About Starting Your Own Mystery Shopping Business But Didn't Know Where To Start?

A popular question I am often asked by both experienced and newbie mystery shoppers alike is "what does it take to start my own mystery shopping business"?

Well, for the answer, I recently had the pleasure of interviewing author and veteran mystery shopping business owner, Shari Joseph who graciously shared her experiences in running her own mystery shopping business, and how you can start one too! Read the interview here:

http://www.mysteryshoppercoach.com/mysteryshoppingbusiness2.html

You can order Shari's book 24/7 using this URL:

http://www.mystery-shopper-business.com/affiliations/mj.html

Plus, if you want to really jump-start your own mystery shopping business, Shari now has a complete kit that contains "plug in your information" contracts, ready made Microsoft® Word questionnaire templates, tracking logs, letterhead, business cards and lots more! Check it out at this URL:

http://www.mystery-shopper-business.com/affiliations/mjKit.html

<u>Please note</u>: I am only recommending Shari's book and kit as the best resources I have seen at a reasonable price for starting your own mystery shopping business. The ultimate decision about whether or not you go into this business rests with you. Please do your own due diligence and check with your legal and other professional advisors on the viability of this business for your own personal circumstances. While I believe the information she has presented to be high quality and reliable, neither I, nor my publishing company can be responsible for any losses incurred as a result of your using the information she has provided.

About Melanie R. Jordan

Melanie left Corporate America to practice what she preaches: achieving a more satisfying and flexible existence with "work that fits her life, not the other way around". Today, based on her business world life lessons, everything she does is only done on her terms.

As a firm believer that the secret to successful self-employment is to have several streams of flexible income, Melanie uses all her talents and experience across a diverse field of self-employed endeavors.

Melanie has 20+ years experience in marketing from her work with some of the country's largest banks, as well as over eight years of experience in direct sales and customer service in the fields of real estate and loans. Her exposure to these two fields led to her establishment of two successful mentoring programs: one for new real estate agents for a small, independent California real estate brokerage, and the other for a national, entrepreneurial marketing and training company in the financial services field.

Melanie is also much in demand as an independent, home-based marketing and infopreneur consultant, sales trainer and coach for small businesses.

However, her biggest passion is writing about, and coaching others on, a variety of topics that she is passionate about related to work-at-home lifestyles, health and fitness, infopreneuring and marketing. She is also the author *of Have Your Cheeseburger And Keep*

Your Health Too! Check out Melanie's other web site "Healthy Eating Coach's Corner" at www.healthyeatingcoach.com for more information about her approach to healthy living. All of her works are published with the in-depth, "tell it like it really is" style, that has attracted fans across North America and in many other countries throughout the world.

She also publishes a free e-zine for mystery shoppers and merchandisers called *The Perfect Work-At-Home Job Update* where she answers select questions from her readers and shares some of her latest tips and news from the trenches (subscribe by sending an e-mail to mscoach@aweber.com).

Melanie welcomes your comments, questions and suggestions and can be reached at Melanie@mysteryshoppercoach.com.

And since she is constantly writing and publishing new books and special reports on a variety of topics, please check her publishing company's web site at http://www.sunloverpublishing.com for other publications you might enjoy.

Printed in the United States
6123LV00002B/168/A